Fremantle Port

National Library of Australia
Cataloguing-in-Publication entry:

Fremantle Port
ISBN   978-0-9805395-3-0 (standard edition)
ISBN   978-0-9805395-4-7 (limited edition - 100 copies)

Conceived, designed, and written by:
John Dowson
Steamship Buildings
10-12 Mouat Street
Fremantle WA 6160, Australia
john.dowson@yahoo.com

Published by Chart and Map Shop, Fremantle
Printed by Everbest

This is John Dowson's fourth book on Fremantle. For details of
Fremantle the Immigration Story (Fremantle Society 2001), *Old
Fremantle* (UWA Press 2003), and *Old Fremantle Childhood* (2006),
please see website at john.dowson.com.au

Fremantle Port

a pictorial history

John Dowson

Foreword

Fremantle Port's bottlenose dolphins display a symbiotic relationship with its big ships. The ships stir gourmet squid from the harbour floor. Squid are a favoured food for dolphins, which also relish body surfing on the bow waves of big ships. Passengers and crew love to cheer them. One sunny day in February 2011, dolphins are hunting and cavorting among a honeycomb of limestone beside the Maritime Museum. This is the last remnant of the persistent bar which C. Y. O'Connor, genius engineer, had to demolish before "the port without a harbour" could get a safe one. *Queen Mary 2* sounds one of her four horns and begins her move off the berth and towards open water. She is the biggest ship to manoeuvre in Fremantle Port's Inner Harbour. The crowd cheers. They cheer again for the dolphins which are now surfing on *Queen Mary 2*'s substantial bow wave. They seem to know they are stars.

Generations of dolphins have seen it all. Seventy years earlier the original *Queen Mary*, with the Anzac landing veteran *Aquitania*, is tossing in the deep water of Gage Roads. Five of the world's fine liners and three cruiser escorts have tied up in the harbour. They soon will be on their way to a war. Dolphins see other things. They see Singapore trader *Sultan* being steered through the limestone gap and into the basic harbour in 1897 by Lady Margaret Forrest. The harbour is open but incomplete. Then there are handsome liners which look like Art Deco posters. Later there are ro-ro (for roll-on-roll-off) car carriers which look like massive steel boxes. How do they move so fast? Below the waterline these boxes become "as sharp as the bow of a tea clipper". Some can carry more than five thousand cars.

After World War Two there are up to three thousand workers on the wharf. They have a special Fremantle name. They are not wharfies but lumpers: they lump cargo. They ride to work on push bikes and in the 1950s, generate the finest football team in Australia. Then suddenly there are only hundreds of port workers and a handful of pubs. Jet passenger planes and container ships have struck….

These are random thoughts about a port which lives on and thrives. My friend John Dowson, devotee of the ocean liner and the glass negative and later digital developments, has distilled thousands of negatives into this coherent love story.

Ron Davidson, author of classic Fremantle Impressions *2007.*

Above: Highnich and newborn August 2011. *Left and previous page:* 1933 liner arrival. *Page one:* 1950s ship arrival.

Contents

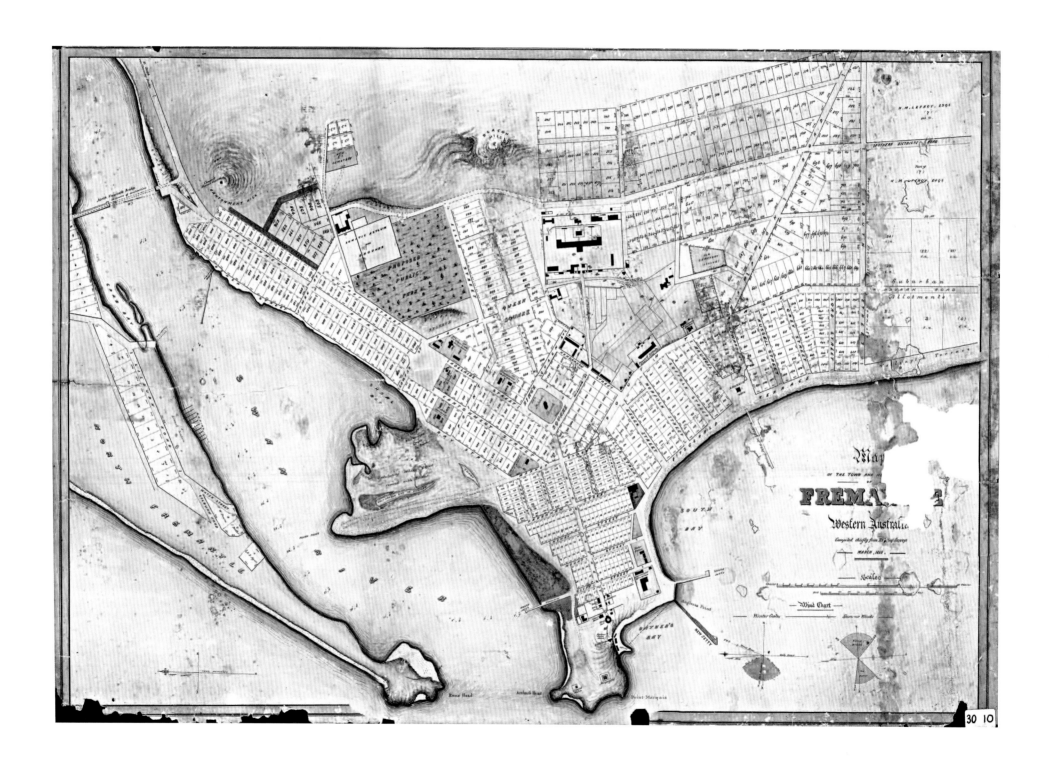

Map
of the town and ...
of
FREMA...
Western Australia
Compiled chiefly from ... Surveys
MARCH 1855
Scale

Wind Chart

30 10

Introduction

This is not a comprehensive history of Fremantle Port. It is a personal exploration of some of the stories that tell that history.

Fremantle is one of the most isolated ports in the world. It often took months to get here. It still takes days to get to the nearest major port. The "First and Last Store in Australia" used to stand on Victoria Quay where the lumpers' cafeteria, the C.Y. O'Connor Centre, was built on the express orders of Prime Minister John Curtin during World War Two. The shop was a reminder of Fremantle's important location - that Fremantle for many was the first they saw of Australia, and for many, the last.

While many ports have altered beyond recognition, or relocated away from their origins, Fremantle Port's Inner Harbour remains in the heart of Fremantle, more than 100 years after its opening in 1897. Besides growth in the volume of trade, the size of ships has relentlessly increased. A recent $250 million dredging will allow its current main business of handling containers to deal with projected growth for years to come.

The current rise in cruise ship visits brings a welcome human face to shipping again in Fremantle, something lost when air travel replaced liners in the 1960s.

The human face can be seen throughout this book in the manpower needed to build the port, the thousands of lumpers required to handle the cargoes, and the endless streams of immigrants, emigrants, general passengers, and tourists hanging off ship railings.

The human face that is not seen is that of the creators of the images, mainly photographs, in this book. Where possible the creators are noted. They deserve our gratitude. Very well known images and ones already used in books such as *Old Fremantle* and *Old Fremantle Childhood*, have been avoided.

Opposite: a very rare, exciting, and never before published map dated 1865. At this time, the Lunatic Asylum, now the Fremantle Arts Centre (left of centre), had just been built, while the large Convict Establishment (coloured pink) in the centre had been operating for ten years. The Recreation Green on the river is clearly shown. This reclaimed land for cricket and recreation was described then as more brown than green. Above that, opposite Bay Street (now Elder Place) is a large protrusion into the river, with samphire, rushes, salt lagoon, and bushes known as Ferry Point. It even has a path marked out, but the area was never developed. Within 30 years of this map Ferry Point was dredged for the port. Fremantle's first bridge is being constructed upriver. Until completed in 1866, it was the site of a convict-manned ferry across the river. In South Bay a watering jetty for ships leads to a well at the end of Arundel Street. The map has been updated post 1872 with a "New Jetty" later known as the Long Jetty.

Left: An 1878 poster featuring the light-house built that year to replace an 1851 one. The poster explains the various signal flags used to show what sort of ship was approaching and where it was. It states: "When the vessel is sighted from Rottnest a blue flag will be hoisted at Fremantle, when she is made out at Fremantle the blue flag will be replaced by the flag of her class."

Figure 4 for example shows a barque from London. Other destination flags shown include Mauritius, Cape (of Good Hope), Sydney, Adelaide, and India.

Early Fremantle

When Janet Millett's ship *Tartar* arrived off Fremantle and anchored in Gage Roads in 1863, there was no jetty at which to berth. She wrote (*An Australian Parsonage* 1872): "As we drew near we saw a scattered little town of white houses, looking like the beginning of an English watering-place, and passed a boat or two rowed by men on whose hats 'Water Police' was inscribed, but the jetty upon which we landed was so lonely and deserted that, with the exception of these amphibious guardians of the peace, one might have supposed that the great jail upon the hill had absorbed almost all the population."

Seven years later, the images on the following pages were taken, still reflecting a deserted looking jetty in South Bay where Mrs Millett disembarked, and an almost totally deserted High Street. The 1870 census shows the total population of Western Australia to be 24,785, of whom 15,375 were males and 9,410 were females. Just over 3,000 people lived in Fremantle. Fremantle's isolation was reflected in the sailing time of 20 days going east to Sydney and 30 days going west to the Cape of Good Hope.

The 1870 panoramic photographs overleaf are arguably the best early photographs of Fremantle in existence. They are not the earliest, as that honour goes to Stephen Stout and Alfred Stone, whose important but less well taken images of Fremantle were produced some five years earlier. The images on the following pages are extraordinary because the original glass negatives still exist, and the detail available is like getting off a time machine in 1870 and walking the streets. High Street runs up the middle of the first picture to the first St. John's church, which faces down High Street to the town gaol, the Round House, near where the photograph was taken - "Heaven at one end facing Hell at the other."

We will take a walk up the 1870 High Street (see next page): The town appears deserted - though there are three people at the corner of High and Mouat and one further up High Street near a pair of carts. This could be 'Paddy,' the wheelbarrow man, who lives in High Street and moves luggage. The first buildings on both sides of High Street after descending from the Round House are the police station and constables' quarters, important in a town where half the adult male population is either convict expirees or ticket-of-leave men requiring surveillance. The large three-storeyed building on the corner of High and Cliff Streets is the residence of Commissary-General Eichbaum - soon to become Mrs Seubet's boarding house for North-West pearlers and rogues like Louis De Rougemont. The offices of the *Fremantle Herald,* run by the former Anglican Dean of York, are on the south west corner of this intersection. Across the road amidst a luxuriant garden, Dr Limon Oliver's wife runs a ladies' seminary, while he has a little chemist shop on the street. Up to the corner of Mouat Street can be seen Castor Oil trees. The southern side of High Street here has a large vacant block growing barley. Crossing Mouat Street we find postmaster Alex Francisco and his general store. Next is well known builder Joshua Harwood's Crown and Thistle Hotel. Across the road is the Emerald Isle Hotel kept by Mrs Marmion.

Walking further up High Street we pass the telegraph office opened last year and run by Mr W. Holman. Before reaching St John's Church, we find another newspaper office, that of the *Era,* published by George Barrow. There is plenty more to see. The Convict Establishment sits above the town and to the right are the large barracks for the pensioner guards. The Freemasons' Hotel is nearby. Back in Cliff Street, the first street running across the photograph, merchant and shipping agent Robert King has his premises open for business. A small dog waits at the gate next door. Walking to the right we find South Bay and South Jetty (pp12-13), with some sandalwood stacked near the jetty and Commissariat. This is Fremantle 20 years before C.Y. O'Connor arrives.

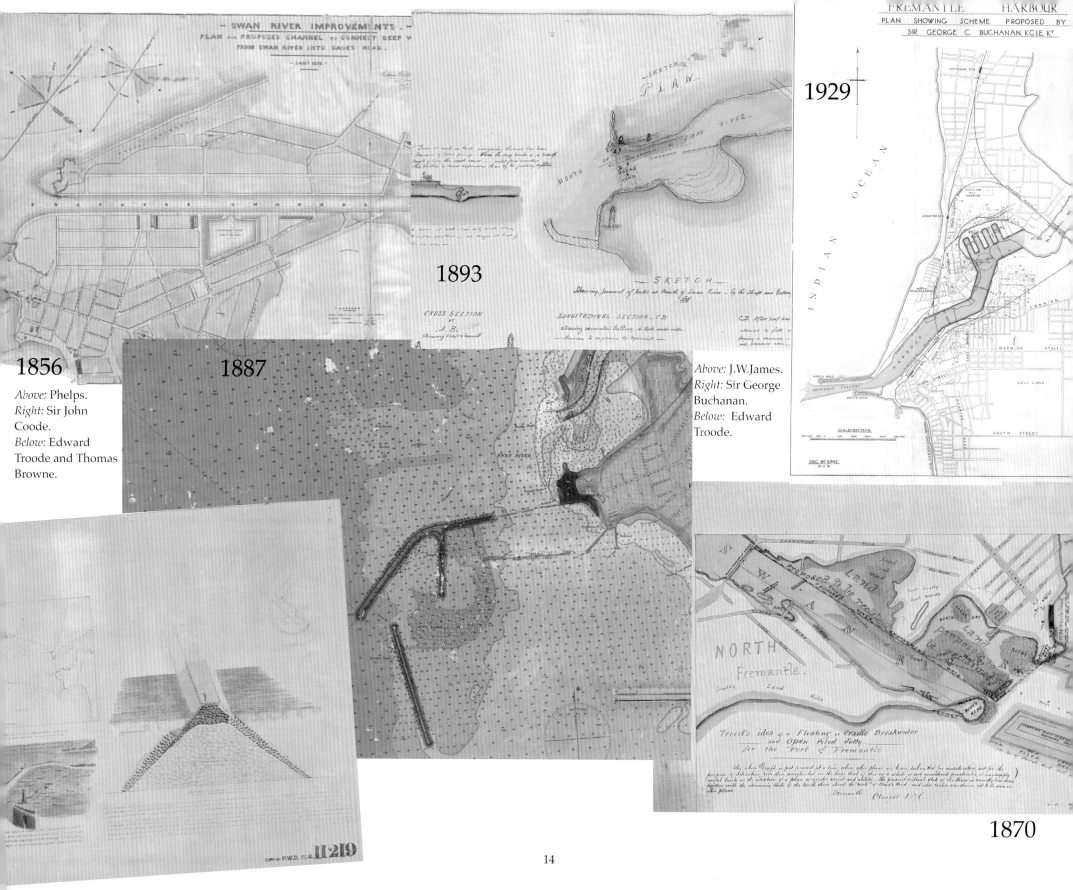

- SWAN RIVER IMPROVEMENTS -
PLAN for PROPOSED CHANNEL to CONNECT DEEP W
FROM SWAN RIVER INTO GAGES ROAD.
- JANY 1856 -

FREMANTLE HARBOUR
PLAN SHOWING SCHEME PROPOSED BY
SIR GEORGE C. BUCHANAN K.C.I.E K.T

1929

1893

CROSS SECTION
AT
A.B.
Showing Shaft & Tunnel

LONGITUDINAL SECTION - CD
Showing excavated Gallery in Rock under water
Previous to explosion by Gun-cotton

- SKETCH -
Showing Removal of Rocks at Mouth of Swan River - by the Shaft and Gallery.

INDIAN OCEAN

1856

1887

Above: Phelps.
Right: Sir John
Coode.
Below: Edward
Troode and Thomas
Browne.

Above: J.W.James.
Right: Sir George
Buchanan.
Below: Edward
Troode.

SWAN RIVER

NORTH
Fremantle.

Troode's idea of a Floating or Cradle Breakwater
and Open Piled Jetty
for the Port of Fremantle.

COPY OF P.W.D. W.A.   II 219

1870

14

Battle of the Plans

1839

Since Fremantle was settled in 1829, there has been no shortage of plans put forward to provide a safe port - at least 25 are known. In 1830 Henry Willey Reveley, in charge of all public works, designed a breakwater for the mouth of the Swan River estimated to cost £165,000, and Governor Stirling advocated a shallow-draft cut channel from the ocean directly into Rocky Bay. In 1837 Lieutenant Jones proposed an angled jetty from Arthur Head. Surveyor-General Roe described a grander version of Jones' idea (see map on left) in 1839. By 1849 there were attempts to open up the bar across the mouth of the river. In 1856 William Phelps proposed a 300 feet channel into the river (see opposite page). while in 1870 Edward Troode thought a floating raft and reclamation in the river would help (see opposite). 1872 saw G. Randell's groyne from Rous Head followed by Thomas Browne's 1875 bizarre dock (see overleaf). The 1875 Select Committee thought a groyne off Arthur Head was the answer. In 1877 and 1887 British expert Sir John Coode devised various groynes off Arthur Head, believing that sand drift would make opening the river unworkable.

In the meantime, the actual works carried out included the South Bay Jetty in 1854, followed in 1872 by a new jetty from Anglesea Point at Arthur Head originally known as Ocean Jetty. It was extended several times, with final work in 1896, and became known then as the Long Jetty.

Ironically, C.Y. O'Connor's harbour, which he had begun in 1892 after some controversy, opened the next year. This rendered the one kilometre Long Jetty obsolete. But there was still much work to be done to the Inner Harbour. In 1913 when the Dominions Royal Commission pointed out that the new Panama Canal would be 40 feet deep, Fremantle Harbour was 30 feet, though by 1920 it had increased to 36 feet deep .

With bigger and bigger ships on their way, plans for port expansion kept coming, with particular emphasis on pushing the port up the river and having ships go to Perth. But, those ideas met resistance. When interviewed by the Dominions Royal Commission in 1913, the Secretary of the Fremantle Harbour Trust Frank Stevens was asked about works that would make the river navigable to Perth for large craft. He replied: "That has excited a lot of parochial trouble." Robert Rolland, Acting Engineer-in-Chief, concurred: "It is advisable not to talk about it."

PROPOSED DOCK AND HARBOUR AT FREMANTLE. W.A.

DESIGNED BY THOˢ

— APRI

N RIVER WITHIN THE BAR. 1875.

ITE OF PROPOSED DOCK. &ᶜ

NORTH FREMANT

LILBU

WATER STREET

NORTH BEACH

PROMONTORY BETWEEN SEA AND RIVER

SITE OF PROPOSED DOCK

This sand bank has been formed by the jutting shore of the promontory
the river but occasioned by the misplacement of the stone Groynes to

Since 1875 the new of this sandbank
has accumulated recently at about 7chains

Sand Bank dries in patches

SWAN RIVER

FERRY POINT

Flat

Sand Bank
dries in patches
at low Water

ROUS HEAD

TRAMWAY

BAR

PROPOSED DOCK AND HARBOUR AT FRE

APR

BIRD'S-EYE VIEW OF GAGE ROADS AND SWAN RIVER MOUTH.

Showing Site of Proposed Dock and Harbour.

Admiralty Soundings in Feet at Summer

GENERAL BLOCK PLAN OF PROPOSED WORKS.

BROWNE. C.E.

75.

W.A.   DESIGNED BY Thos H.J. BROWNE. C.E.

DRAWING Nº 1.

NORTH FREMANTLE

LILBURN ROAD

STREET

RIVER

P.W.D. W.A.
II 219
9

— BIRD'S-EYE VIEW OF PROPOSED HARBOUR WORKS.

Shewing Ferry Point reduced and levelled, a Bridge thence to Dock, and Canals cut between Sea Work and River.

To be reclaimed and filled in

FERRY POINT REDUCED

Drawn from prev
By Thos H. J
Fren

Suggested site for
Railway Station

SWAN

BAR

LE

The Long Jetty

Promenading on the Long Jetty c1907. The new harbour has been open for ten years, but along with the recently completed swimming baths at the beginning of this jetty, and bandstand in the adjacent new Esplanade Park, this was a popular place to be seen. Even the rail lines have been removed. Before Fremantle Council decided to take responsibility for the jetty, *The West Australian* noted on August 21, 1904: "The Harbour Dis-Trust has decided to close the long jetty at Fremantle....The jetty was for a long time the happy hunting ground for suicides from the Old Men's Depot."

The only known early photograph of camels in Fremantle, despite their regular use there during the gold rushes of the 1890s. These camels are shown on the end of the Long Jetty, about to be loaded aboard the Howard Smith Ltd 2,070 ton coastal vessel *Buninyong* for the Murchison.

River Views

Above is an important image from a now demolished lighthouse showing a great deal about Fremantle and the Swan River in the late 1880s, just after the railway station was built on what was Fremantle's recreation space, Fremantle Green. In the right foreground is the 1850s Government Cottage which survived until the 1960s. Across the image runs Cliff Street to the North, or River Jetty, in the Swan River. Goods came along Cliff Street from South Bay or from across the bar in lighters from ships moored in Gage Roads, to be loaded for shipment to Perth. The railway and passenger bridges can be seen in the background. No harbour works have yet begun inside the river mouth. On the left of this page is a detail from an even earlier (1870) image, reproduced in full on earlier pages, showing part of the Recreation Green and the original foreshore.

Passmore's Fremantle

Over the page can be seen the detailed and accurate embroidery Henry Passmore produced c1890 of the river with which he was so closely involved. A one-legged Crimean War Royal Navy veteran, he arrived in Western Australia in 1865. By 1872 he was in charge of convicts on public works, including 20 convicts working Western Australia's first dredge nicknamed *Governor Hampton's Yacht*. The Colonial Secretary Malcolm Fraser quipped: "You will be able to say you commanded the first ship the Western Australian Government owned." Reconstructed by 1888 she became known as *Black Swan* and worked at the mouth of the river until C.Y. O'Connor arrived in 1891 and refused to allow convict labour in the building of the new port.

Passmore lived in John Street, North Fremantle. The embroidery looks from North Fremantle across the river. Passmore's dredge *Black Swan* is in the lower left with the *Priestman* grab dredge to the right in front of the pilings intended to keep the dredged channels open. Over the river, the buildings shown are accurately placed. The 1880 railway station with its sheds that obliterated the Fremantle Green is in the centre, to the left of the North or River Jetty. Arthur Head has its 1878 lighthouse and signal mast, with ships at the Long Jetty behind. The limestone bar at the mouth of the river is clearly shown, with a narrow passage either side. Why Passmore chose embroidery is interesting, but his elder brother did work in a lace factory in England. This well preserved artefact is a superb reminder of the Swan River at its mouth just before harbour works commenced in 1892.

It is tempting to suggest that this is possibly Henry Passmore c1890 on Rous Head supervising convicts carrying out his work there of planting fig trees to arrest sand drift. The uniformed man has his back to a dredge in the Swan River which is the *Priestman No. 1*. Passmore came back to Fremantle after 1886 following five years battling sand drift in Albany. In 1872 Rous Head had been stripped of its vegetation to make fascines to fill a breach the sea had made between the ocean and the river. Passmore used convicts stationed there: "In such parties there was invariably some weak ones, old age, or feeble ones, to be given light labour; these were employed in planting fig trees." (*The West Australian*, Nov. 12, 1912)

The Bar

Captain Charles Fremantle took possession of Western Australia for the British on May 2nd, 1829. On May 1st his diary records problems getting into the river: "found it impossible to enter from the excessive sea on the reef or bar extending from point to point."

One of the great Fremantle stories is that of the coralite limestone bar across the mouth of the Swan River and how it saved the river, and Fremantle. In ancient times the river had turned left at the mouth and flowed through what is now known as the West End. A channel dug through there would have been easier than Captain James Stirling's and others' idea about a channel from the sea to Rocky Bay. But, once buildings were erected east of Arthur Head (the place where the Round House now stands), that possibility disappeared.

The bar across the river prevented all but the smallest craft from entering the river. It prevented ships from bypassing Fremantle and sailing directly to Perth. It meant that ships had to unload outside the river.

Surveyor-General Roe provided the following sailing directions in 1840 for Gage Roads off Fremantle: "When abreast of the east end of Rottnest which is distant 9 and a half miles W.N.W. from the mouth of Swan River, the flagstaff and low white jail on Arthur's Head will be easily distinguished, and the vessel will be boarded by a pilot.... A safe and convenient berth will be found in somewhat more than 6 fathoms water a mile from Arthur's Head....The Harbour Master and Pilots are prohibited anchoring vessels in Gage Roads between the 1st of May and 1st of October, on account of the westerly gales which sometimes distress the shipping there during that period, and have driven some on shore. ...Owen's Anchorage offers a secure retreat from Gage's Roads during winter." His advice for crossing the bar at the mouth of the Swan River was: "Observe that the deepest part of the channel is close to some detached cov-

ered rocks which lie to the north of the South head. In steering for the channel, keep rather towards the South head, until you bring a black cross beacon (near the sandy beach inside the south head) and the black gable-end of a house a little beyond it, in a line with a large heap of stones on the outline of the hills over the town of Fremantle...These three marks in a line will lead over sandy ground, close on north side of the covered rocks off the south head, and clear of a larger ledge which points inwards from the north head. The depth of water between the two is 5 to 7 feet, according to the time of tide." Early port regulations stipulated that if the bar was considered unpassable, a ball would be hoisted on the yard-arm at Arthur Head as a warning. By 1868 a £10 fine was threatened to ensure adherence to the warning.

Efforts were made to enlarge the small channel on the north of the river entrance near Rous Head, and some maps show the shallow passage as Trigg's Passage, after Henry Trigg, Superintendent of Public Works, who tried to blow up the bar in 1848. The Board on the Navigation of the Swan River, which had Surveyor-General Roe as its President, twenty years later was still trying to improve entry in to the Swan River from the ocean and to improve navigation channels. By the time C.Y. O'Connor was using a ton of dynamite a week in the 1890s to remove the bar to allow ships into the river, the passenger and railway bridges had been built across the river in Fremantle. The railway bridge was later rebuilt further upriver, but it was too difficult and expensive to move the passenger bridge. Thus was the Swan River saved.

Looking west down High Street from the tower of the Fremantle Town Hall c1890. The mouth of the Swan River and the bar across it can be seen above the tower of "Manning's Folly," a large building intended to be a resort hotel for Indian officers. Very little of this pre-gold rush architecture remains. The 1878 lighthouse on Arthur Head was demolished in 1905 to make way for gun emplacements.

Plans: Coode v O'Connor

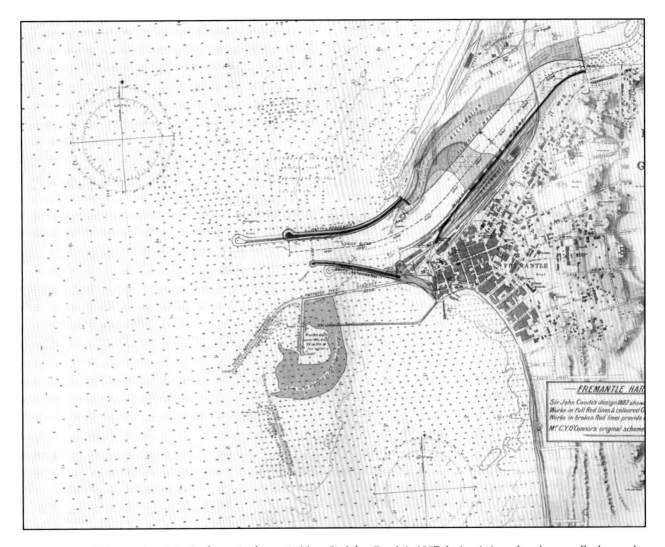

Above: C.Y. O'Connor's original scheme is shown in blue. Sir John Coode's 1887 design is in red and green. Broken red lines indicated possible future works. Coode, first consulted in 1875, felt that sand drift made a river port too difficult.

Opposite: Harbour Master George Forsyth's painting of the Harbour Master's boat under sail off Fremantle. The vessel was used as a pilot boat and for general harbour duties. The flag being flown from the mizzen masthead appears to be his fanciful variation on the defaced blue ensign. Forsyth was Harbour Master from 1874 until dismissed in 1886. Forsyth's godfather, the eminent English cartoonist George Cruikshank, helped him with his art before he went to sea at the age of fourteen. Other Harbour Masters like Charles Russell and E.J. Miller were also very competent artists.

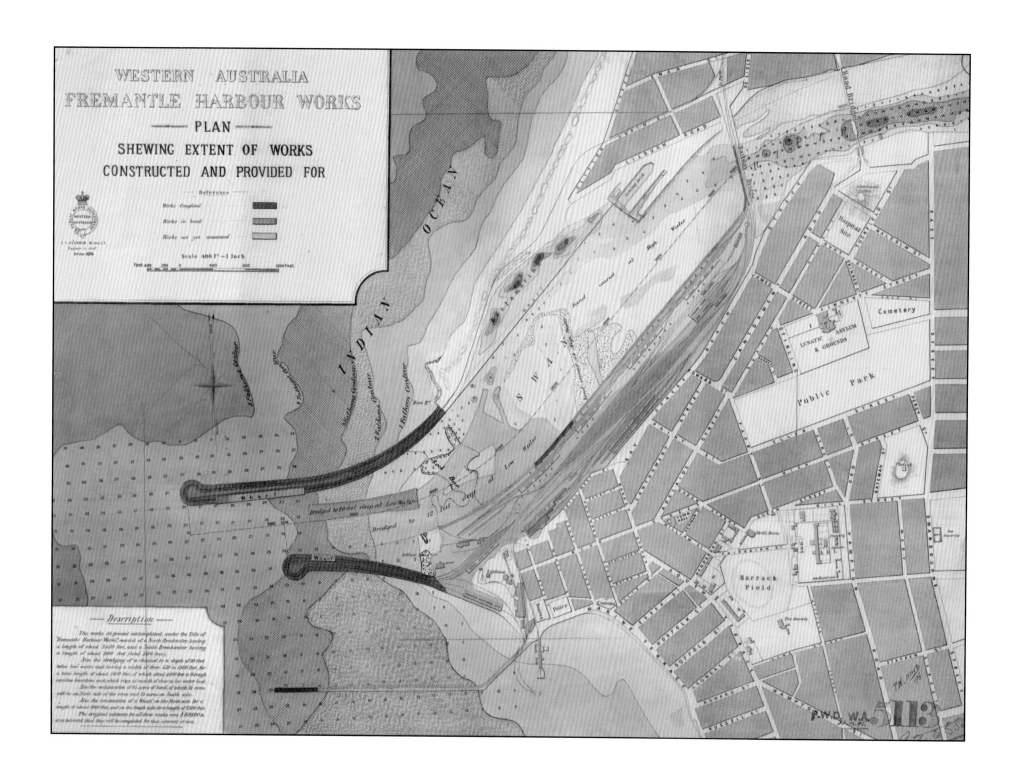

C.Y. O'Connor: Building the Port

When C.Y. O'Connor arrived in 1891 to take up his appointment as Engineer-in-Chief, he soon decided that the new harbour should be inside the Swan River. He did not agree that such a choice would cause problems with sand drift, as raised by engineers like Sir John Coode. He had met, among others, Henry Passmore, who later wrote: "I was camped at Rous Head when Mr. O'Connor was considering the different schemes. In conversation he mentioned this fact of sand travel, which was denied by me. He said: 'Have you not read Sir John's report?' I replied, 'Yes I have, and notwithstanding this report there is no sand travel.' The day being very calm and the water like glass, I said 'Come I will prove to you there is no sand travel. I will show you the rocky bottom, the holes in the rocks, the seaweed growing in these holes, the limpets on the rocks also. If there was any sand travel you would see nothing of the kind.' He went with me in a boat. I asked him to fix his eye on the bottom, and he would be able to see what I said. The boat was pulled slowly, so as not to disturb the surface of the water. I am convinced he could see the bottom to 20 or 30 feet. On lifting his head he said, 'Where were you when Sir John Coode visited the State?' I replied, 'At Albany. Who gave him his information I could not say.' Mr. O'Connor was quite convinced there was no 'sand travel.' On the next day he brought Sir John Forrest that I might show him what I had shown Mr. O'Connor the day before." (*The West Australian*, Oct. 15, 1912)

In a report dated December 21, 1891, O'Connor dismissed another in-river option of a channel through the narrow neck of land opposite Rocky Bay because: "If the railway had not to be crossed twice, and the main road also twice, the state of the case would be materially different."

In early 1892 Parliament approved O'Connor's plan for opening the bar and constructing a harbour at the mouth of the river. It was estimated that £800,000 would be needed for a basic harbour. All along O'Connor received fierce support for his river plan from his Minister, Harry Whittall Venn, the State's first Director of Public Works and Commissioner of Railways. Until Venn was sacked

in 1896 when phenomenal growth resulted in railway blockages, they achieved a great deal together, not only with Fremantle Harbour, but in the development of railways that fed the port. Providentially, the gold rush boom, and the financial independence of Responsible Government in 1890, allowed further allocation of large sums of money for the projects as they progressed.

The north and south moles were constructed of limestone from Arthur Head and Rocky Bay until the deteriorating quality led to supplies being sourced from Boya. Reclamation of some 20 acres on the north of the river and 54 on the south proceeded with the building of a retaining bank from end to end, 10 feet above the water level and 20 feet wide. By August 1896 the government issued orders to commence wharf construction, leading to 1,500 feet of quay being available for vessels by June 30, 1897. But the depth of water alongside was only 20 feet. A wharf was built on each mole in 1897 to meet demand, the tough jarrah piles being driven straight into the limestone moles. In 1900 a jetty projecting into the harbour from the north quay was designed to attract mailboats, as it was feared they may not get away fast enough from the south quay during high winds. In the end, the mailboats, the greyhounds of the sea, berthed at South Quay, later Victoria Quay.

Additional works included a slipway, breakwind, and lighthouses. The slipway at the base of North Mole was a timber structure (see overleaf), especially useful for repairing the four dredges, which otherwise would have had a voyage to Melbourne. The wooden picket breakwind of 2,200 feet east from the base of North Mole provided protection from north-west gales. Two lighthouses were erected on Rottnest, with a third at Woodman's Point. The 1878 Arthur Head lighthouse was gone by 1905, but South Mole had a lighthouse erected in 1903 and North Mole in 1906, with a temporary wooden one there from 1901 (see page 67).

Opposite: Fremantle Harbour Works commenced in 1892. This October 1896 map shows works constructed and those planned. Works in red had been completed, works in hand are in lighter red and works to be done are in pale pink.

Building with Jarrah

Enormous quantities of timber were used to build Fremantle Port. The government was keen to see the vast resources of the forests thus used. However, the timber did not prove to be as sturdy as originally thought, with the jarrah continually being replaced due to attack by the marine mollusc teredo navalis. Early reports on the value of Western Australia's "mahogany" (jarrah) said it was impervious to attacks: "Our colonial boats with mahogany planks below the bends, lie the year round in our harbour, unhurt by the 'teredo navalis,' though the same insect unsparingly devours heart of oak close by; nay, it seems destructive to the very barnacles, which foul a ship's bottom so much." (John Schoales Jnr. in *Report on the Statistics of Western Australia*, Perth 1841).

Captain Stirling's HMS *Success* had been repaired in 1829 at Fremantle using jarrah. When the ship was broken up in England, the workers were so impressed with the condition of the jarrah, they sent a report to the Lords of the Admiralty, who commissioned an order for the Portsmouth dock of "200 loads of thick stuff." The order was never filled, as the struggling colony did not have the manpower. But it was recommended that a port be built fifteen miles south of Fremantle at Peel for steamers going between Cape of the Good Hope and "Eastern Australia." and from there Western Australia's "unlimited" timber could be exported.

Above right: c1902. Looking upriver from Victoria Quay. Seated on the edge of the railway line, a bearded gentleman looks up from reading his newspaper.

Right: Colonial tender SS *Penguin* on wooden slipway at North Mole.

Opposite above: Drilling holes for explosive charges to blast limestone bar..

Opposite below: Harbour construction showing reclamation works.

A ton of explosives was used each week in the quarrying at Rocky Bay and during the removal of the limestone bar across the river mouth. On January 1, 1895 an explosion so loud it could be heard in Perth was the final straw for locals, and a deputation arrived at Premier John Forrest's office three days later. The group bemoaned the lack of safety standards for explosives. They said that it was quite common in Fremantle for men to go into a merchant's store and buy gunpowder by the keg, empty it into a bag and carry it along the railway. Nine out of ten got into a smoking carriage, and the bag, as a rule, was put under the seat.

John Forrest shared the concerns, noting that: "Not knowing very much about explosives, he had perhaps a greater fear of them than those who understood them better. But he did not think it safe to carry on blasting operations with so much explosive material stored in the vicinity." He ordered the explosives to be taken away in an old schooner *Laughing Wave,* and moored off Woodman's Point. The man using all the explosives, C.Y. O'Connor, was at the meeting, and agreed that "there had been somewhat slipshod arrangements in the past."

Another explosive issue which arose during the construction of the harbour was the arrival of bubonic plague into Australia. After an outbreak in Hong Kong in 1894, there was concern it would arrive in Australia through shipping routes. The first plague death in Australia was on January 19, 1900, in Sydney. Then, in April 1900, nineteen-year-old William Campbell, at Fremantle No. 1 goods shed unloading cargo off the *Pilbarra* and *Marloo* from Sydney, was stuck down with the plague. He died within three days. There being no crematorium in Fremantle, he was buried at sea. People stopped eating fish.

At this time, further widening of the main wharves led to problems, including that of colonies of rats living among the stonework, providing a source of danger. The problem was solved by using a concrete face to some of the stonework.

Although hundreds died in Sydney in a series of plague outbreaks, around seven succumbed in Fremantle. The fear caused by these outbreaks led to dramatic and rapid improvements in public health. Along with this, on January 1, 1903, the Fremantle Harbour Trust came into being to control all aspects of the port.

Explosive Issues

C.Y. O'Connor's port gradually moved up the river towards the railway bridge and the house he rented above in Beach Street overlooking the Swan River. That, and other grand houses running down to the river (top) went. One of O'Connor's eight children, Kathleen, took art lessons from the Harbour Master Charles Russell. While Russell left behind competent and historically important paintings of Fremantle, Kathleen looked further afield for her inspiration: "I don't think the harbour would be a good subject for a painting," she told the *Daily News* on April 1, 1950. "You must put ships in paintings of harbours - and I've never painted a ship which looked like a ship." A pity, because by August 2011 one of her paintings had sold for $198,000.

Opposite: Driving timber piles for berth construction.

The First Fremantle Bridge

Dredges

Rare view of the Fremantle traffic bridge soon after completion by convicts in 1866. Only a handful of Fremantle photographic images exist from this period. This one emphasises the important new connection across the river, allowing much better access to Perth, and opening up North Fremantle and Mosman Park.

The building of this bridge stopped large boats going upriver once the limestone bar across the mouth of the river was removed 30 years later. The 1880 railway bridge downstream (despite Coode's recommendation it go upstream of the traffic bridge) prevented the port's expansion until a new railway bridge was built nearer the traffic bridge in 1964. Despite various plans to build docks and ship facilities upriver, it was too expensive to replace the bridges. This is the bridge that saved the Swan River.

The first bucket dredge bought by the government arrived in sections in 1869 and was assembled in North Fremantle. Worked by convict labour, the *Black Swan* dredge was used up and down the river and to remove sand banks inside the bar at its mouth.

O'Connor used the bucket dredger *Fremantle* (far right), which had arrived from England in October 1894. In January 1896 the suction dredger *Premier* worked on sand inside the river. Between 1893 and 1901 some 8.32 million cubic yards of dredgings were dumped north of the North Mole.

The relentless increase in the size of ships, while providing more economical freight, has necessitated repeated dredging.
Opposite below: Ladder dredge leaves Fremantle Harbour 1927.

WHARF. FTLE HARBOUR. 1800.

1893: Major reclamation works in the Swan River are underway. The suction dredge *Premier* is pictured. Her spoil is pumped through the pipe just beyond her. While the *Sultan* gets credit for being the first ocean going steamer to enter the Swan River, on May 4, 1897, it should be noted that on October 28, 1896, Captain Reid had his 40 ton coastal schooner *Theresa* towed into the river through a fifteen foot deep channel, to berth at the "railway jetty." The *Theresa*, which was built in the Swan River, is thus the first trading vessel to berth at a wharf in the Swan River. The first vessel to use the wharf on the North Mole was the *Andania* from the Intercolonial Steamship Co fleet, which discharged 3,000 tons of Newcastle coal there on April 29, 1897. On land, the importance of the railways is clear to see. On the opposite page, in 1899, the new wharves on reclaimed land are full, just two years after the official opening of the inner harbour.

C.Y. O'Connor- The Great Chief

Fremantle Harbour in the making

When O'Connor's port was opened in 1897 he was out of the State planning his next major work - the water pipeline to the goldfields. When his Coolgardie Water Supply Scheme was opened in 1903, O'Connor was not there either. He had committed suicide ten months earlier. The great works O'Connor carried out as Engineer-in-Chief were inter-related and helped Western Australia leap into a new century. The new Fremantle Harbour needed the railways; the new gold towns and the railways needed the water; and Western Australia needed the transcontinental railway.

Charles Yelverton O'Connor needed support and help too, but when he needed it most, he didn't get it. The very man who had made the harbour happen, was gone. The brilliant engineer suicided during a blistering heatwave on Monday, March 10, 1902. Dogged by vicious attacks in the *Sunday Times*, in the midst of a Royal Commission into his Goldfields Pipeline scheme, and with his mentor John Forrest away, he had had enough.   *Above:* 1897 workers. *Opposite:* c1905 driving sheet piling for berth construction .

Open for Business

In 1897 Fremantle Harbour opened for business. This image is 1904.

On its March 1899 visit, SMS *Saida* is the first foreign man-of-war to enter the new Fremantle Harbour. This Austrian training ship had 300 officers and men. During its stay of several weeks, the Premier John Forrest invited officers to a picnic at Mundaring to hear Western Australia's Engineer-in-Chief C.Y. O'Connor explain his other great engineering feat - the beginning of the goldfields water pipeline scheme. Forrest extolled O'Connor's virtues and said that the pipeline was: "the greatest work which the colony had in hand, and probably the greatest work of its kind which had ever been undertaken on the whole of the Australian continent." During the *Saida*'s extended stay, O'Connor accompanied ships' officers to Coolgardie. During one function to honour the guests, Forrest announced that North Mole would be extended 1000 feet. *Above and above right*: SMS *Saida* was open to the public several times while in port.

Port Visitors

Japanese warship 1903. Thousands visited the ships but a disorderly group led to the *Matsushima* being cleared of visitors. Japanese warship visits became at times contentious, though in World War One, the Anzacs were escorted to war by a Japanese warship. There were two issues: firstly the new White Australia Policy, and secondly the suspicion that Japan was rising too quickly as a world power. In 1910, the Japanese Squadron visited Fremantle with two cruisers *Aso* and *Soya*, which had been captured from the Russians. The Japanese commander Rear Admiral Ijichi had to give precedence to one of the 150 naval cadets on board as the cadet, Imperial Highness Prince Kitashirakawa, was the nephew of the Emperor. In a secret report to London, the Governor of the time, Sir George Strickland wrote: "The feeling against the Japanese had been aroused in the State during the Federal Elections, which had just concluded, by a candidate remarking in a speech- that, if the SS *Pericles* (recently lost at the neighbourhood of Cape Leeuwin in Western Australia) had been commanded by a Japanese, she would not have been wrecked. The candidate was assaulted on the spot, his meeting broken up, and he himself very severely injured. Just before the arrival of the Japanese, sensational reports appeared of refusals to take part in a Guard of Honour for the Japanese Admiral." But, the visit went well, and the Colonial Office noted that the Governor "seems to have shown tact."

SS *Perth* c1905. By 1902, many harbour workers had been laid off and unemployment around town was evident. But, in 1902 Fremantle overtook Albany both in the number of ships visiting that year (410 v 248) and total tonnage (1,045,170 v 540,910). The year O'Connor arrived (1891), Albany had ten times the tonnage and 203 ship visits compared with Fremantle's 58. The government was accused of secretly spending £60,000 to buy land to extend the harbour upriver to Rocky Bay, but the bridges got in the way of that plan. Another plan, put forward in 1902 by the state's most prolific architect, George Temple-Poole, showed two miles of wharf built for ships along the South Perth foreshore in Melville Water, with spoil from dredging the river used to fill in Freshwater Bay. Fortunately, nothing eventuated.

Opposite: Ships of wood and men of steel. Wooden sailing ships require constant upkeep. One crew member is holding a wooden plane, another has a paint-splattered shirt, while others are attending canvas sails.

Above: Unloading coal at the Fremantle Power House, South Mole, on June 19, 1905.
Opposite: The Public Works Department building surveils the harbour entrance c1900. This was C.Y. O'Connor's construction office, built in 1893. Relocated to 1 Cliff Street in 1904, it was in use till demolished in 1962. Paddle tug *Gannet* tows in a sailing ship. Was C.Y. O'Connor watching from an office window?

RIVER ENTRANCE FREMANTLE. W. A.

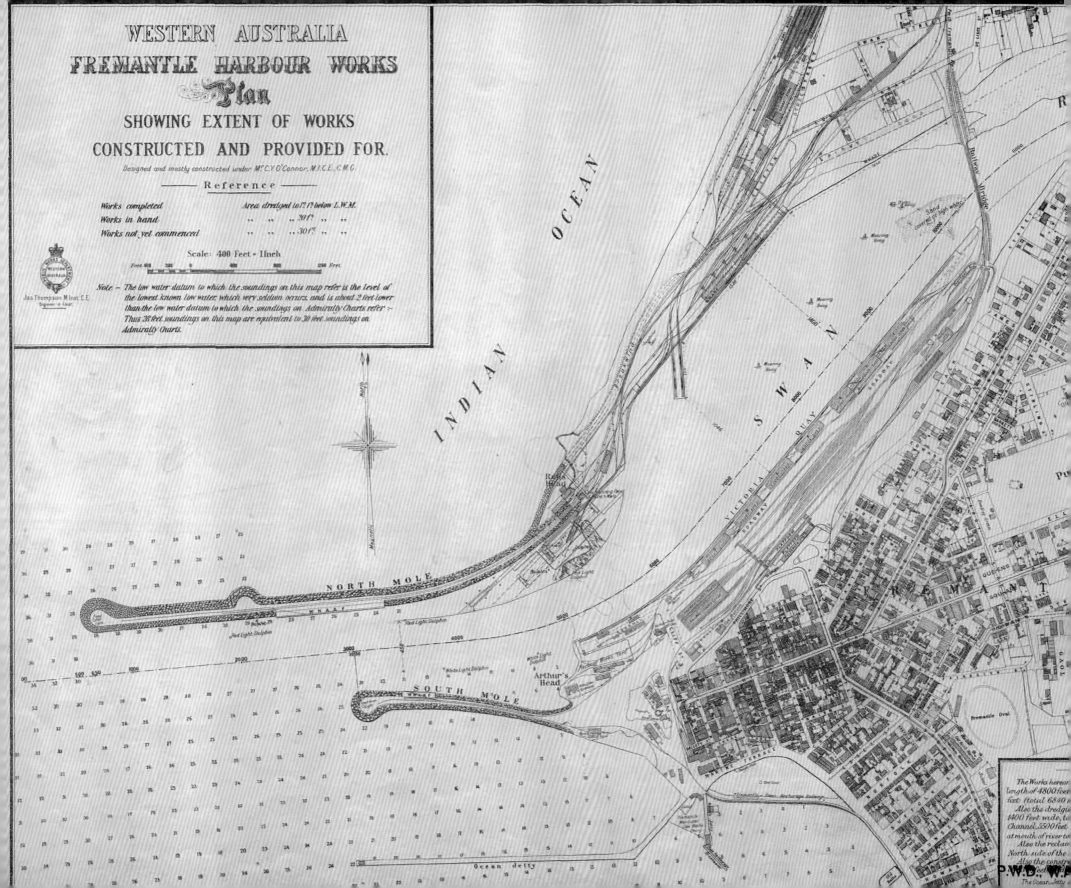

WESTERN AUSTRALIA
FREMANTLE HARBOUR WORKS
Plan
SHOWING EXTENT OF WORKS
CONSTRUCTED AND PROVIDED FOR.

Designed and mostly constructed under Mr C.Y.O'Connor, M.I.C.E., C.M.G.

— Reference —

Works completed	Area dredged to 12 ft below L.W.M.	
Works in hand	,, ,, 20 ft ,, ,,	
Works not yet commenced	,, ,, 30 ft ,, ,,	

Scale: 400 Feet = 1 Inch

Feet 400 200 0   400   800   1200 Feet

Note — The low water datum to which the soundings on this map refer is the level of
the lowest known low water, which very seldom occurs, and is about 2 feet lower
than the low water datum to which the soundings on Admiralty Charts refer :—
Thus 28 feet soundings on this map are equivalent to 30 feet soundings on
Admiralty Charts.

Jas Thompson M Inst. C.E.
Engineer in Chief

North

INDIAN   OCEAN

SWAN   R

NORTH MOLE

WHARF

SOUTH MOLE

WHARF

Arthur's Head

Red Light Dolphin

White Light Dolphin

FREMANTLE

Fremantle Oval

VICTORIA   QUAY

Ocean Jetty

The Works hereon
length of 4800 feet
feet (total 6840 ...
Also the dredgi...
4400 feet wide, ta...
Channel, 5500 feet ...
at mouth of river ...
Also the recla...
North side of the ...
Also the const...
The Ocean Jetty ...

P.W.D. W.A.

Moving Along

Top: c1912. Daly Bros delivering wool. Wool was a major export. Dalgety's held their first wool auction in 1912 and Elder Shenton their first in 1914. In 1915 they and C.H. Fielding & Co formed a wool association.
Above: Original Public Works Department offices being relocated in 1904. In use by Harbour Trust until 1962.
Opposite: A very useful 1908 Harbour Works plan, updated in red to show progress made in the previous few years with port development and the extraordinary number of new buildings in Fremantle resulting from the gold rush boom and increased business. The proposed dock shown at Rous Head was later abandoned after £200,000 expenditure . C.Y. O'Connor's chosen site below the railway bridge was not used due to lack of a proper foundation. The Rous Head site had similar problems. They even discovered a cave there.

Above: Well known tug *Awhina* operated as a working tug during the week, and here as an excursion vessel on a weekend. *Opposite:* This 1901 photograph has EVERYTHING - small vessels and large, steam boats steaming, sailing vessels sailing, a paddle steamer, yachts, railways, and even a large anchor. In the middle sits the Swan River Shipping Co. paddle tug *Nirimba* which towed lighters to the Barrack Street Jetty in Perth. The 2,710 ton steamer *Gulf of Ancud* had a fire on board when in Fremantle in 1898 - the harbour works steam launch *Black Eyed Susan* helped on that occasion. In 1900 the captain and owners were awarded £5,000 for rescuing the steamer *Darius* and in 1901 they rescued the crew of the *Jessie Nicool*.

Blood, Sweat and Tears

The port provided a wide range of employment opportunities. Cargo handling was carried out by lumpers, who were hired on a casual basis, generally by the day. While this suited ship owners and the widely fluctuating trade flows, it made it difficult for lumpers and their families, did little for harmony on the wharves, and deterred efficiency increases. The Fremantle Lumpers' Union had been formed in 1889 and numbers grew to 843 by 1918 and 1,624 by 1929. The Fremantle Harbour Trust (FHT) had a monopoly of cargo-handling on the wharves from 1904 and employed half the total workforce.

Though by the late 1920s the FHT had sixteen three ton gantry cranes and six others of two ton capacity, cargo handling in Fremantle was still very much a manual operation. Working conditions and facilities for lumpers were primitive. When World War One broke out, a lumper's wife wrote to Frank Stevens, Secretary of the FHT on November 9, 1914: "The time as come that us wife's as to come forward to ask you to help us get our husbands work to feed our children be kind enough to ask your foremen to pick up some of the men that has not done much work for a time...you do not know the state of our homes or you would feel quite sad us women try and do our best and with the help of you might save a few tears these bad times."

By the beginning of the 1930s' depression, the annual accident rate for lumpers was almost 40%. Unemployment during the depression peaked at 28.7% in 1931-32 and led to fierce competition for jobs on the wharves, with the development of the system where strong men known as 'bulls' would set the pace for work to be carried out. Until the Americans arrived in Fremantle with their mechanical muscle during World War Two, Fremantle Port remained a backbreaking workplace, often mixed with blood, sweat, and tears.

Right: A lumper pauses to mop his brow.
Opposite: Loading timber sleepers in 1910 on the finger jetty at the North Wharf. Jarrah, karri, and wandoo were used for sleepers. Over 90% of the "endless" jarrah forests of Western Australia were cut down for utilitarian purposes like beams, columns, wharves, bridges, railway sleepers, and street paving blocks. Jarrah sleepers had an average life span in WA of 25 years, or 40 years in New Zealand's climate.

Sandalwood

Sandalwood, an aromatic wood prized particularly by the Chinese and Indians and used mainly in joss sticks as part of religious ceremonies, has been a significant export since 1844.

A trial shipment aboard the colonial schooner *Champion* to Bombay in 1844 realised prices double that obtained for timber and whale oil. Sandalwood mania gripped the colony for a few years, with the value of the product almost equalling that of wool in 1848. But the boom collapsed by mid 1849. The sandalwood trade picked up again, with 9,605 tons exported in 1882, but the wood had to be sourced further away from the initial area of the Avon Valley.

The gold boom in the eastern goldfields and improved transport led to a sandalwood boom from 1896 to 1911. In 1890 the W.A. Distillery Company of London set up in Albany to extract sandalwood oil, but the company soon disappeared. Elsewhere in Western Australia sandalwood oil was produced, and it was used medicinally as an antiseptic and cure for venereal disease. The highest export quantity ever was in 1919 when 14,355 tons were exported.

The first four images on these two pages appear to be from that boom period c1919. They detail the story of cutting and stacking the wood into enormous piles before shipment.

The demand for joss sticks continues to grow, and Western Australia, home to the largest sandalwood resource in the world, still has a healthy sandalwood export market.

The Adelaide Steamship Company's 3,664 ton *Yongala* steams out of Fremantle c1908. Built 1903, the *Yongala* arrived in Fremantle that year for the Sydney to Fremantle passenger run. She disappeared, without trace, in 1911 after leaving Mackay in Queensland with 73 crew and 47 passengers. She was discovered in 1958 in twelve fathoms near Townsville.
Opposite: E.G. Rome's oft published 1907 view of loading sandalwood at North Mole is so good, it can be published again here.

SS *Grosser Kurfurst*

Grosser Kurfurst first arrived in Fremantle in December 1900. The Premier and Lady Forrest were entertained on board by Captain Remkasten.

At the time, *Grosser Kurfurst* was the largest liner to prowl the seas between Europe and Australia, and the biggest to use the Suez Canal - so big she raised concerns with the Canal Company.

Ship travel was growing in popularity with the choice of comfortable steamers available from British, French and German companies. And a new activity was bringing more people to Australia - tourism.

The ship was seized by the United States during World War One and served as a troopship under the name USS *Aeolus*.

Norddeutscher Lloyd Co's 13,182 ton liner was the second largest vessel in its fleet of 108 ocean steamers, 28 river steamers, and 115 other vessels.

Right: On board scenes (top to bottom): Ladies Salon, First Class Dining Room, Forward Passage, The Promenade Deck.

The Australian Station

HMS *Powerful* arrived on 29 November 1905 and moored at No. 2 buoy in the river. Before entering the river Admiral Fawkes used his gunpowder to give a seventeen gun salute to HMS *Euryalus*, already in port. HMS *Powerful*, 14,200 tons and with a complement of 838 men, carried twenty four twelve pound guns and two submerged torpedo tubes. She relieved HMS *Euryalus* as flagship of the Australian Station. The London Military and Naval Record (December 1905) commented: "She is a most expensive ship to run, owing to her immense coal bill, and she will prove the most costly flagship that has ever been assigned to the Australian station."

Above: A romantic soul took a day time photograph from the light-house and turned it into a postcard of Fremantle Port at night.

Left: Norman Lindsay sketched a boat pumping water whilst transiting Fremantle in 1909 on his way to London aboard the new Orient Steam Co. ship *Osterley*. Years later, in 1932, at the height of the Great Depression, when he was in Fremantle on his way back from overseas aboard the mailboat *Mongolia*, the press asked him about the art market in Europe. He told them that: "Art had crashed all over the world." *The West Australian* commented: "If this be true Mr Lindsay's disgusting pictures and those of that crank Epstein are very largely responsible for the fall."

Top: Barefoot boys with fishing rods eye a passenger wrestling with his luggage c1905.
Above: Robert Robinson's Daimler being loaded in Fremantle Harbour 1908 for a trip to the Eastern States. Robinson had formed the Albany law firm Haynes & Robinson in 1889 and later entered parliament. He helped establish the Albany Woollen Mills in 1925.

c1905 Looking from the North Wharf finger jetty towards Victoria Quay, with the city behind. The town hall can be seen behind the barque. The King's Drink St. Emil sign is behind where the 1907 Fremantle Post Office would later be built. The tall building to the right of that is "Manning's Folly" a large building at one time intended to be a holiday resort for British officers from India. On the jetty, filled with well-suited people fishing, three children and others watch a pipe-smoking man bending over, with what hopefully was a worthwhile catch.

RMS *Moldavia*

When launched in 1903, *Moldavia* was the largest vessel ever built for P&O. At 10,000 tons, she had 350 first and saloon, and 170 second class passengers, and a crew of 340. On arrival in Fremantle, inspections were invited, for a fee. The Captain also sent out one thousand invitations for an At Home on board. The trip to Ceylon took ten days. *The Western Mail* on October 1, 1904 described life on that journey: "There is no harm in pointing out that a modern mailboat is very like a Noah's Ark. The humans vary as much as Noah's animals....and any attempt to bring them into one group must result in a compromise of some sort. There is nothing more curious to notice than the way in which people sort themselves out on a steamer.... Meanwhile the steamer goes swiftly on its way, through an ocean that borrows its glories from the sky.... One wonders why deck games never vary, but the monotony of sea and sky answer this question, and the eye wanders from face to face, noting the vacuous expressions of the players, their open mouths, dull eyes and listless movements.... The ladies complain of the damp heat, because it takes their hair out of curl, and gives their heads a dowdy appearance."

Sir John Forrest, Premier and later Federal Member, used *Moldavia* regularly. In 1908 as he was being farewelled *The Western Mail* commented : "A writer in a paper had waxed wrath with him for having compared Fremantle with Brindisi, that ancient port in Italy. Well he had given up Brindisi long ago; the comparison now was with San Francisco - the golden gate of the West."

Above: Two years before O'Connor arrived in Fremantle (via Albany) this 1889 Orient Line schedule shows Albany as the main port of call for Western Australia. Begun in 1877, the Orient Line by 1889 was running eight steamers on the route and charging from £52 10s for a first class ticket from London (Tilbury). On August 14, 1900, Orient Line's *Ormuz* was the first British mail steamer to call at Fremantle. By 1919 P&O had a controlling interest in the company.

Fred's Voyage 1905

Nineteen-year-old Fred Taylor was sent on a voyage aboard the Queen Margaret *in 1905 to broaden his experience. He left New York on September 10, and was in charge of the ship's slops. He also acted as ship's chemist. He took the photograph on the right. And, he kept a diary:*

Wed Dec 20: We began to smell the land breeze yesterday and it is fine. It is so different from the salt air.

Thurs Dec 21: We have not made more than 2 knots the whole day. Tonight we saw the light which is on Rottnest Island; we should surely sight land tomorrow!

Fri Dec 22: It was very hot this afternoon.... A little before two bells this afternoon, a cry of "Land Ho! Dead Ahead!" told us that we were nearly to the "promised land"... I am quite proud of myself, as I have worked up every sight since October 9th. The Captain has not worked them at all. At the same time we sighted land we sighted two three-masted barques to windward of us, making for Freemantle. We soon could see the lighthouse and then the pilot boat making out to us. As soon as we got a tow-boat, the sails were furled; I going up to help.

Sat Dec 23: The tug came out to us again early this morning and by noon we were moored to the wharf. We are really in Australia!

Fred photographed his way from New York to Fremantle. The image (above right) is important. Firstly, it shows the 1901 wooden lighthouse on North Mole that was replaced in 1906 with a permanent one. Secondly, Fred was pioneering the use of an Eastman Kodak Box Brownie camera which he bought for $1 soon after they were first released in 1900 - a product which revolutionised photography by making it available to a mass market. He used it well.

Queen Margaret

"There can seldom have been a more stupid and unnecessary end to a ship than that of the beautiful Queen Margaret*"-Basil Lubbock*

A fast and beautiful four-masted steel barque built in 1893, the *Queen Margaret* came to a wasteful end on May 5, 1913, following a 108 day voyage from Australia to Lizard Point off the Cornish coast in England. On the opposite page she is pictured in Fremantle c1908, while above she is pictured in 1905.

Queen Margaret had to sail close inshore to receive the owner's signals about where to take the cargo, to get the best price. Ship radios were not then commonplace.

The ship hit a rock and stuck fast. After several days, the cargo of wheat was swollen, splitting the hull and deck open. *Queen Margaret* was a total loss. She sold as salvage for just £50.

Railways

When the railways arrived in Fremantle they robbed the Portonians of their riverside open space, the Recreation Green. But they got a lifeline out of town, after a "Battle of the Plans" decided that the rail route should go north of the river rather than south. The Fremantle to Perth line opened on March 1, 1881 with a railway bridge downstream of the passenger bridge rather then upstream as suggested by engineer Sir John Coode when he submitted plans for the harbour. The bridge celebrated its completion when a special train crossed on August 31, 1880. A station built then at the end of Cliff Street was the western most terminus in the country.

As the railways in Fremantle grew, they made access to the port more difficult. In places a dozen set of lines had to be crossed to get to the wharf. By 1904 the cramped railway workshops had gone to Midland, but even a new station at the end of Market Street in 1907 led to grumbles that port access was still tortuous. But, the port could not have grown and flourished without the freight carrying capacity the railways provided.

Right: 1907 image of locomotive running sheds which commenced operation on November 25, 1905 and survived until 1965. Prominent is the sleepened bank of the elevated coal stage, with the 25,000 gallon water tank and the steam crane working the coal grab. The building alongside the turntable housed a boiler to heat up water for washing out locomotive boilers. The running shed is full of locomotives of the N,G, and K classes. To the left of the shed a suburban train heads off with an N class locomotive. The lead cars are small side door compartment cars from the 1890s, while the others are from 1903-1905. The photograph looks south-west towards Princess May School and the Australia Hotel.
Below: Fremantle's first railway bridge with an N class locomotive hauling a suburban train c1900. The bogie van behind the locomotive is a W class used for perishables like meat and milk. The train is approaching the four navigation openings, two of which collapsed on July 22, 1926, suspending train services for three months.

E.L. Mitchell captures fit, determined, and confident Western Australian soldiers embarking for war in 1914 - a war that became increasingly serious, and whose effects were felt for decades. The most famous writer to have spent childhood years in Fremantle, Xavier Herbert, recalls seeing his brother off to war when he was thirteen: "I had the deeply affecting experience of seeing Phillip off across the world to war....I fought my way to the barricade and climbed to the top of it, to perch on the pickets. It was the biggest ship I'd ever seen, the *Medic*, a famous old White Star Liner of the Atlantic run. Then, miraculously, there was my brother, my prince, right before me, perched on the ratlines of the second of four high masts. I stood balanced, waving, yelling. Of course he could not hear me in the din. But at last he spotted me. I went mad. He waved and laughed a bit. Then he buttoned up his face, raised a hand to his mouth, and yelled at me. He need not have added the gesture of dismissal, because I'm positive I heard the order above the uproar, that order I knew so well: "Nick off!"

World War One

Two years after photographer Ernest Mitchell showed the confident and fit Western Australians going to war, he captures (above) the first wounded arriving back in Fremantle. Wounded but unbowed, the injured men pose on the deck of their ship, one soldier with an eye patch, jauntily smoking a cigarette. The wounded later included Lawrence McCarthy, a Victoria Cross winner, who spent time in the Base Hospital in South Terrace next to the synagogue. Lawrence, born in York, was hailed in the British press as a "Super VC" for destroying five German machine guns and taking 50 prisoners. The prisoners even carried him back to his unit on their shoulders. Historian Charles Bean wrote that, next to Lieut. Albert Jacka at Pozieres, his "was perhaps the most effective feat of individual fighting in the history of the AIF."

1918. The war ends. The survivors return. Anzacs are seen marching from the port entrance down Cliff Street. 34,000 men enlisted in Western Australia, of whom 32,231 went overseas. Only 23,670 returned. From Fremantle itself 3,714 men and women embarked, with 2,872 returning - 842 Fremantle sons were killed in the war. Among those embarking in Fremantle on the *Medic* with Phillip Herbert (see previous page) was John Simpson, a fireman off the coastal vessel *Kooringa*, who went on to be the famous "Simpson with the donkey" at Gallipoli. His love of animals extended to a pet possum which he took with him on the *Medic*.

Wheat

The port of Fremantle has many layers of history that constitute a fascinating storyline of endeavour. There are extensive trails leading to and from the port, often no wider than the deck of a ship or the width of a railway line, bringing goods to the port and taking them away. One of the major cargoes handled at Fremantle for many years was the annual wheat harvest.

This backbreaking work required each gang of twelve men to load 2,800 bags a day, each one weighing up to 95 kilos. Western Australia's wheat harvest increased rapidly in the 1920s when the photographs on these pages were taken, from 340,000 tons (1921) to 1.4 million tons (1931). Bagged wheat caused bottlenecks, with up to eight vessels loading simultaneously and each one taking a week. But the government was nervous about introducing bulk handling, as by 1929 the world was in the grip of the Great Depression, and 60% fewer men were needed for bulk handling. That would have resulted in significant job losses among the 280 men loading grain at country terminals and the same number on the wharves. Bagged wheat would later give way to bulk wheat and costs plummeted 50%. The first shipment in bulk (1932 on the *Maplewood*) actually involved workers taking bagged wheat off the gantries, slitting them open and pouring the wheat into the hold.

Co-operative Bulk Handling Ltd was set up in 1933. In 1934 it sued a newspaper for alleged derogatory reports about storage methods. But Agricultural Department inspector Harold Rudall said he had seen mould in bulk and bagged wheat, with some bags "growing whiskers" as the grain sprouted. A 1935 Royal Commission into CBH's monopoly found that the producers' co-operative could continue.

Fishermen of Fremantle

Italians from Capo d'Orlando in Sicily and Molfetta in Apulia were pioneers of the Fremantle fishing fleets. In 1891 when C.Y. O'Connor arrived, there were only 36 Italians in the whole colony. The gold rush and poor conditions in Italy led to 150 Italian fishermen living in Western Australia by 1898. To help control the industry, a market shed was built by the Public Works Department on South Jetty in 1908. But it was run by Fremantle Council in a way that antagonised the fishermen. It took until 1947 for a co-operative, not unlike what the wheat growers and market gardeners had, to be formed with the guidance of Paddy Troy, Secretary of Fremantle Trades Hall. The Co-operative's Fish Market, though greatly altered, still stands near Bathers' Beach as the home for various food outlets. Above, the children seem distracted as an impressive local catch is displayed c1910.

Italian fishing boats in the Fishing Boat Harbour April 11, 1933.

Bloody Sunday

Top: Fremantle Lumpers' President William Renton with Alex Panton MLC following Renton's wounding during the wharf dispute.
Above: A large crowd gathers dockside for Tom Edwards' funeral.
Opposite: Lumpers and tally clerks.

The Fremantle Wharf crisis of 1919 resulted in the death of lumper Tom Edwards when he was struck going to the aid of Lumpers' President William Renton. The incident shone a light on the unsatisfactory work practices on the wharves, which continued through the next war as well.

Trouble on the wharves had been brewing for a long time. During the war, in 1917, the Fremantle Lumpers' Union (FLU) refused to load a Dutch ship with flour, fearing it would end up in the hands of the enemy. The Commonwealth Government, in charge of shipping matters at the time, guaranteed employment to the National Waterside Workers' Union (NWMU), which it had helped set up. On April 12, 1919, the FLU refused to allow the *Dimboola*, initially quarantined due to the serious Spanish flu outbreak, to be unloaded. The State Government intervened, as the ship had urgently- needed supplies. The Premier of Western Australia, Hal Colebatch, having taken office on April 17, after the dispute began, went downriver to supervise the police who had taken possession of the wharf. His launch was attacked with scrap iron and stone when he passed under the Fremantle bridges. Thousands of people were milling around - including lumpers, their wives, and ex-servicemen - some of whom had access to revolvers. After shots were fired at police, there was a police charge, during which Tom Edwards was fatally injured. A conference between the Premier, Police Commissioner, and lumpers' officials led to the withdrawal of the official party. Alex McCallum, secretary of the Labour Federation, worked to pacify the lumpers. Non-union labour left the wharves. Writer Xavier Herbert, who himself had been a "scab" during the war on the wharves, noted: "To most of us, the revolution was really only a one-day affair."

Left: Minister for Works and Member for South Fremantle Alex McCallum turning on the tap to discharge the first bulk spirit cargo from SS *Radex* on North Wharf, April 8, 1927.

Below: McIlwraith, McEacharn & Co's interstate liner SS *Karoola* c1922.

Opposite: From November 23, 1923 until September 24, 1924, the 48,400 ton HMS *Hood* and the Special Service Squadron made a 38,152 mile Empire Cruise as a reminder that Britain still ruled the waves. All ships berthed in the harbour, the first port for three months where that had been possible. Enormous crowds visited the ships, though matters were not made easy when many people boarded HMS *Hood* with their own refreshments, and settled down for the afternoon. One lady, lost in the seemingly endless, immaculately presented ship, breathlessly asked a bluejacket: "Where is the sea?" Meanwhile, the Admiral, with his own Rolls Royce on board, was able to escape for a few hours.

HMS *Hood* 1924. It took two years to build, two years to fit out, and two minutes to sink, in World War Two. There were three survivors from a complement of 1,415 men.

HMS *Hood*

HMS *Renown*

The Fremantle visit of the Duke and Duchess of York aboard HMS *Renown* between May 18 and May 23, 1927, was the end of a long tour of Australia which began with a welcome from a million people in Sydney. After opening Parliament House in Canberra on May 9 they had a rough passage across the Great Australian Bight. The Duke, who went on to be King George VI between 1936 and 1952, and the Duchess, who was to return here as the Queen Mother, received a rapturous welcome. The sentiment of such visits at the time is reflected in the following:

"Above the coo-ees of farewell there arose in the wake of the departing warship a tumult of loyal acclamation that floated up above the water to their Royal Highnesses, waving adieu from the hurricane deck. Steaming out between the national guard of honour of the north and south moles, black with people, the warship caught the echoes of that burst of cheering as it was picked up and carried by the people to the last extremity of land, where the last fluttering flag marked the outpost of the people of Australia, and the last loyal cheer, caught up and carried softly on the breeze, was to their Royal Highnesses, gazing on the receding scene, the last voice from Australia, and the epitome of a great farewell. "(*West Australian*, June 2, 1927)

Upper right: Royal couple. *Right and opposite*: HMS *Renown*.

81

People Smugglers and Cofferdams

Fifty Chinese men from Hong Kong were found by customs officers in the ballast tank of the *Almkerk* when she arrived in Fremantle in November 1927. Pictured here is their ship and their transportation to court in a Metro bus. The spicy newspaper *The Mirror* ran a screaming headline: "World's Record Haul of Chinese!" In its words: "50 Chinamen, dirty, unkempt, and struggling for breath, were dragged from the bowels of a ship at Fremantle." The 50 men had paid people smugglers for passage from Singapore to Fremantle and had been promised work on arrival.

Right: Resident engineer-in-charge of Fremantle harbour works from 1934, Cyril Morgan had worked in the port since 1919 when extensive replacement of jarrah piling due to teredo navalis attack was carried out. Here he has photographed a cofferdam (South Mole in the left background) being constructed c1922 as part of building a slipway for the construction of the new hulls for the dredges *Fremantle* and *Parmelia*.

RMS *Strathnaver*

In the depths of the Great Depression, P&O's latest luxury liner (opposite) arrived in Fremantle for the first time on November 2, 1931. A crowd of 3,000 assembled. The Premier Sir James Mitchell and others were given a tour of the ship. The P&O representative from London on board, A.W. Gent, said he paid a penny halfpenny a mile on the English railway for transport only, whereas by using a tourist class ship it was possible to be transported, housed, and fed across half the world at the cost of well under one penny a mile. But, a lack of new orders meant unemployment for 900 of the workers who had built *Strathnaver* and her sister ship *Strathaird* in 1931.

Both ships were 22,000 tons, were advertised as "the largest electric vessels in the world," had the latest amenities like talkies (movies), kept spare propellers at Bombay and Sydney, and came with a new, all white colour scheme, reducing the internal temperature by four degrees Fahrenheit. In both, the first and third funnels were dummies - removed after the war (in which they were troopships).

Right: Ship arrival 1933.

World War Two

Wartime events in Fremantle, while heavily focussed on getting service personnel to and from distant battlefields, for the first time had a distinct local significance. The threat of Japanese invasion was real, and the arrival of highly mechanised Americans in Fremantle from 1942 meant that Fremantle was not just a transit stop, but a real place that needed defending. Australians were now defending their own interests, with new allies by their side, and were moving away from the eurocentrism of just helping a British homeland. Fremantle Harbour is noteworthy for its defence contribution, and this theatre of war makes the place one of great heritage significance.

On the right sits the 42,348 ton RMS *Empress of Britain*, in Fremantle, fitted out as a troopship. On May 12, 1940 she left Fremantle in a troop convoy with the *Empress of Canada, Aquitania, Queen Mary, Mauretania*, and the *Andes*. In October 1940 she was attacked by German bombers and a submarine, and sunk off the coast of Ireland. A grand liner built to sail for Canadian Pacific from UK to Canada, she was launched during the Great Depression in 1931, and was the largest liner ever to sail regularly between two ports of the British Empire.

Opposite: The navy moves in.

Above: 1940: Now demolished causeway to the wharf, with anxious family and friends farewelling troops to war.
Opposite: December 1939. World War Two, and hectic embarkation for combat on the other side of the world.

World War Two: The world's greatest ships carry Australians to war and back

Troopships

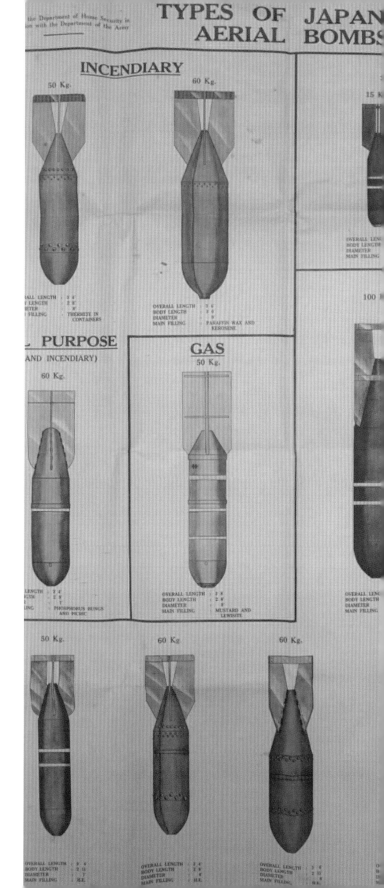

Above: Troopship *Sontay* arrives October 18, 1945 with 1,063 mainly Air Force personnel from India and Burma.
Right: By 1942 the fear of Japanese attack on Fremantle led to extensive defence measures and large civil defence posters like the one on the right. The poster features possible gas attack. The US 7th Fleet, which occupied the old asylum (now Fremantle Arts Centre) installed a gas chamber there to prepare for any such gas attack.

Opposite above: February 18, 1943. Return of 9th Australian Division from the Middle East. Prime Minister Curtin wanted the 9th Division back from their successful campaigns, to defend Australia. Code named Operation Pamphlet, the whole 9th Division, all 31,451 of them, was brought back in four great liners: *Aquitania, Queen Mary, Nieuw Amsterdam,* and *Ile de France,* with *Queen of Bermuda* as an armed merchant escort carrying 1,731 of the troops. The liners were also armed, *Queen Mary* having 66 anti-aircraft guns and a gunnery crew of 100. In the photograph opposite above, *Nieuw Amsterdam* on the left is entering Fremantle Harbour and *Queen Mary* is berthed in Gage Roads. *Nieuw Amsterdam* entered the harbour with 6,241 troops and 465 crew. Australian war correspondent and poet Kenneth Slessor was on board. He found the Indian Ocean crossing rather warm. He described sleep in his cabin as "like being slowly asphyxiated in a bath of hot glue." *Opposite:* 1942 convoy.

RMS *Queen Mary*

The *Queen Mary* menu above featuring the *Georgic* on the cover shows what the Australian officers ate for luncheon the day before their convoy sailed on May 12, 1940. A year later, the author's mother embarked on the *Queen Mary* as a VAD nurse. Her diary recalls: "Embarked *Zephyr* but returned after hitting *Queen Mary* as too much swell ....waited Fremantle sheds until 4.15am and got out ship about 6am. QM most marvellous interior like lovely ballroom."

Luncheon

Hors d'Œuvres, Varies

Potage Dauphine

Fried Fillets of Blue Cod, Remoulade

Noodles, Pomodoro
Frankfurters and Sauerkraut

Roast Fresh Pork, Savoury and Apple Sauce   Mashed Parsnips
Baked Jacket, Puree and Lyonnaise Potatoes

To Order From The Grill:
Minute Steaks, Rockaway

Cold Buffet
Fresh Brawn   Roast Lamb
Bologna Sausage   Pressed Beef
Melton Mowbray Pie   Derby Round of Beef

Salads
Tomato   Potato
Lettuce   French Dressing

Tapioca Custard Pudding
Ice Cream and Wafers

Cheese   Coffee

1941. One of the greatest ships of all time: *Queen Mary* in Gage Roads, all 81,237 tons of her. Built by John Brown & Co of Scotland, she had her maiden voyage on May 27, 1936, just three years before war broke out. A passengers' favourite, she had a notorious roll, which, according to one crew member: "Would roll the milk out of a cup of tea." First arriving off Fremantle in April 1940, she made the trip to Sydney in 3 days, 6 hours and 42 minutes, averaging 28.5 knots. Her great war record, along with other great liners converted to troopships, possibly shortened the war by a year, according to Sir Winston Churchill.

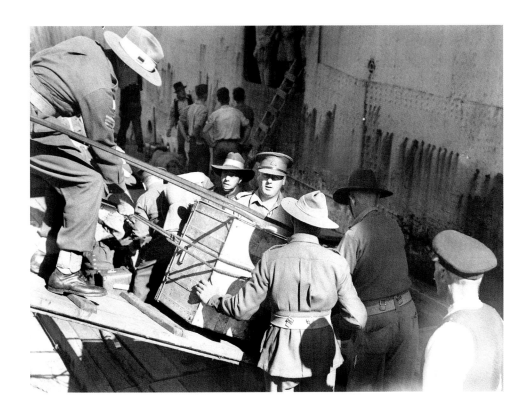

Great liners became great troopships. *Queen Mary* (nicknamed *Grey Ghost*) visited Fremantle nineteen times between May 10, 1940 and March 26, 1943. Above, crates of money are being loaded aboard *Queen Mary* to pay troops. *Queen Elizabeth* made eleven visits between May 10, 1940 and December 10, 1941. *Aquitania* beat them both, making a total of 22 visits during the war.

"My brother Frank had gone overseas in the *Queen Mary* before, with the airforce. My parents came to say goodbye - we could see each other through a wire fence. You never knew if you'd see each other again. Think of all those women living for three or four years without any male help, their family lives all topsy-turvy: young women in the land army; petrol rationing; clothing coupons and all that. Those were the days of making clothing from curtains. Living with the fear that your men would not return, or come back so different you would hardly recognise them. " (*Author's mother Joan Dowson MBE OAM VAD, who went overseas on the troopship* Queen Mary. *Her brother never returned.*)

Above: Pool with a mother-of-pearl ceiling, and gymnasium aboard *Queen Mary*. Despite refitting for wartime, the pool remained, as Joan Dowson recalled: "Most lovely swimming pool - with promenade on top - simply glorious." In normal times the gym, featuring seven different timbers, was equipped with horse and camel riding machines and vibrating chairs and belts.

RMS *Aquitania*

RMS *Aquitania* was launched in 1913, not long after the sinking of RMS *Titanic* with the loss of 1,513 lives. 100,000 people attended the launch. *Aquitania* had her maiden voyage a day after the RMS *Empress of Ireland* sank with the loss of 1,012 lives, and a year before her sister ship RMS *Lusitania* was sunk by a German submarine, with the loss of almost 1,200 lives.

The only liner to serve in both world wars, *Aquitania* transported 25,000 wounded in WW1 and served as British troopship in the Gallipoli campaign. She transported 400,000 military in World War Two. *Aquitania* also picked up 26 of *Kormoran*'s crew after its battle with HMAS *Sydney*, going against orders not to stop for survivors of sinkings. The last liner to operate with four funnels, she was scrapped in 1950 after a glorious career spanning 36 years.

Aquitania's 22 visits to Fremantle as a troopship give her a special place in Fremantle's maritime history. Is she the greatest ship to have ever visited Fremantle?

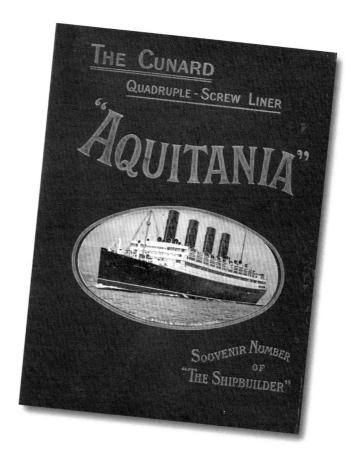

Opposite: Boom defence vessel HMAS *Karangi* ferries troops ashore from troopship *Aquitania* on November 22, 1945. *Aquitania* had left Liverpool with 4,639 passengers. At Fremantle, 213 Western Australian members of the RAAF, four AIF former prisoners of war, and 229 South Australian members of the RAAF disembarked. *Aquitania* returned on December 14 and disembarked 1,046 service personnel. This was the last time the great liner visited Australia.

EUR 274M,60 — LARGEUR 29M,60 — PROFONDEUR (du pont des embarcations) 28M,20 — TONNAGE BRUT 47,000 TONNEAUX — VITESS

NOEUDS – HAUTEUR JUSQU'AU SOMMET DES CHEMINÉES 50^M. – HAUTEUR JUSQU'AU HAUT DES MÂTS 67^M. – ACCOMMODATION PO

SECOND CLASS DRAWING ROOM

Over Here Boys

During World War Two, a new signal station was established on June 14, 1944 on top of the North Fremantle grain silos (above). From their vantage point, in October 1945, WRAN A. Borthwick is signalling and WRAN H. Bruce is writing.

During the war, an average of 300 ships a year were repaired in Fremantle, often involving difficult underwater work due to inadequate drydocking facilities. United States, and later British and Dutch, submarines crowded the port. Civilian workers on US submarines had to go on a test dive to prove the seaworthiness of their work. The Americans welcomed the British submarines, as a British Top Secret file (Kew ADM 199/509) reveals: "Rear Admiral Christie welcomed the prospective arrival of submarines smaller than the US submarines, which had proved unsuitable for operations in the shallow waters of the Java and Flores Seas...In general, the equipment, facilities and amenities provided by the US Navy for the Base and submarines are on a most generous, in fact, lavish, scale, far beyond anything that would be expected for a similar British organisation....It is considered unlikely that British and US ratings will mix much as they will be on such an utterly different financial level."

Of note during wartime was the repair of the Dutch Shell tanker *Ondina* in Fremantle, which, though badly damaged, had sunk an enemy Japanese merchant raider with a tiny four-inch gun. *Ondina* went on to fulfil a vital role in the allied submarine operations from WA. The State Engineering Works and private enterprise were vital to these repairs. But, ship berthing was problematic, with 40% of the wharfage space permanently occupied by allied navies. Harbour Trust employees were kept busy, especially the pilots, with one pilot bringing in seven ships in one day.

Opposite: United States submarines crowd North Wharf.

Above: 1945. The fire aboard the MV *Panamanian* was one of the port's most dramatic incidents ever. On a blistering hot January day in a harbour packed with warships, merchantmen, submarines, and support ships, MV *Panamanian* was loading flour at North Quay. A smouldering rag thrown overboard ignited the wharf and the ship. The first fire brigade engine to arrive was engulfed in flames. The 8,900 ton depot ship HMS *Maidstone* with a load of torpedoes and ammunition caught fire and was towed away from the wharf where her fire was extinguished. The fire aboard the *Panamanian* took several days to burn out. The Fremantle Harbour Trust was sued but won the case.

Post war Fremantle. A wet wharf welcomes those from afar. From above, Frank Hurley captures popular migrant ship *Johan Van Oldenbarnevelt*.

Migrants

Fremantle has always been a place for migrants. The first migrants found life hard and often moved on to other colonies. Almost 10,000 forced migrants, convicted transportees courtesy of Her Majesty's Government, arrived in Fremantle between 1850 and 1868, mainly housed in the now World Heritage listed Convict Establishment. The public works their labour produced provided meat to the skeleton of Fremantle, no work more so than the 1866 bridge across the Swan River.

Immigration soared during the 1890s gold rush. The peak year was 1896, with 55,215 arrivals and 19,324 departures. By 1903 Western Australia had, for the previous ten years, an excess of immigrants over emigrants of 139,131. This excess was vastly greater than any other state, the nearest being New South Wales with an excess of 1,127.

In 1901 the Immigration Restriction Act, the 1903 Naturalisation Act, and the 1904 WA Factories Act aimed at restricting non Europeans (the so called White Australia Policy was abolished in 1958). Europeans, however, were flooding into the USA, and in 1907 the USA absorbed 1,285,349 European migrants, while the total immigration flow into Western Australia that year was just 1,139.

In 1906 an immigration and information building was built on Victoria Quay, and by 1912 it was relocated between C and D sheds, where it survives today, albeit in a largely altered form.

Migrants during the gold rush generally got their equipment and headed east to Coolgardie and Kalgoorlie. When the gold rush petered out, the government encouraged British migrants to come and farm the land. New arrivals were marched from the ship to the Immigrants' Home in South Terrace next to the synagogue, though the heckling they received along the route resulted in the introduction of covered waggons. Immigrants received free board and lodging for three days.

After World War One, immigration was considered vital for agricultural expansion, and the Group Settlement Scheme brought several thousand British settlers. The Fairbridge Society and Dr Barnado's Homes thought the most easily assimilated migrant was the young one, so very young children were brought to Western Australia. There were temporary wartime immigrants when 500 children arrived on the *Batory*, evacuated from Britain. After the war, in 1949, Prime Minister Chifley stated: "We must populate Australia as rapidly as we can before someone else decides to populate it for us."

The vast majority of migrants to Australia arrived after 1945. Between 1945 and 1977, at which time official migrant traffic was switched to air, 169 vessels made 2,000 trips to Australia carrying three million people. For most, Fremantle was their first sight of Australia.

Below: Mr and Mrs F.J. Cornes and family arrive as migrants on March 31, 1950. *Opposite:* Child migrants 1947.

Previous pages: Panoramic view from North Wharf taken in 1946 just after the war. The cargo ships still have mounted guns.

Left: Late 1940s, when the Swan River really was the swan river.

Above: Fruit exports c1958. Black Swan apples are on their way.

Adelaide Steamship's coastal steamer *Mundalla* (3,018 gross tons) was in service 1926-1959. Here she is pictured on June 3, 1959. In 1932 the ship's master was charged with speeding in Brisbane harbour. *Mundalla* had a narrow escape from a British mine inside the Great Barrier Reef after the war, in 1947. Dislodged during a cyclone, the electric mine was spotted just in time for the ship to veer to port. One of *Mundalla's* cargoes from Fremantle was arsenic from the Wiluna mine, the last such cargo being in 1948. By 1950 the average cargo per ship being unloaded in Fremantle was 1,000 tons compared with 200 before the war. That and the large cargoes carried by interstate ships led to the "Rottnest Queue" of ships waiting to get into the harbour. The *Mundalla* was now needing six days in port instead of the earlier three, even with 1,400 waterside workers on the wharves.

Frank Hurley's View

Frank Hurley's extensive career in photography included six trips to the Antarctic between 1911 and 1931, coverage of both world wars, 320,000 km travelled in the Middle East during the 1940s, and a 400,000 km photographic odyssey around Australia between 1946 and 1956. The aerial views on these pages and overleaf were taken in 1950. Flying was his greatest love: "Oh, the exhilaration of the upward climb" his 1918 diary reveals.

1950: A busy harbour has a beautiful white beach just metres from it. Victoria Quay over the river has extensive rail freight running right onto the wharves. On the left of Victoria Quay, the lighthouse tender *Cape Otway* sits outside another ship. To the right of it is the interstate passenger ship *Kanimbla*. In the middle of the harbour the tug *Wyola* is escorting a freighter. The Stateship *Koolinda* is behind. On the slipway is the tug *Una*. The city behind the wharf is fronted in part by large woolstores. On the far left behind one of the woolstores, the former lunatic asylum still has large sheds in front and a laundry building behind, from the US 7th Fleet occupation during World War Two. The wooden footbridge in the centre leads from the immigration building on the wharf across to the railway station, with buses looping and loping around Pioneer Park.

After taking the photograph on the previous page, Frank Hurley's plane swings around the harbour entrance to look back (north west). The freighter from the previous picture has now cleared the harbour and tug *Wyola* peels off from her escort duty. We see the nascence of the Fishing Boat Harbour. Beyond the Fishing Boat Harbour groyne can be spotted remnants of the demolished Long Jetty. The bandstand in the Esplanade Park has been replaced with a flagpole.

1960s

Above left: Russian research vessel *OB* in 1967, well supplied with local lager, and its own aircraft.

Left: The converted tanker *Escape* was loaded with 26,300 tons of bulk wheat for China from this facility in August 1963. The bulk handling terminal worked day and night to load the wheat and claimed a national record for the biggest cargo of grain ever loaded at an Australian port.

Opposite: A very busy and full harbour 1966. Tugs *Wilga* (left), *Wyola* (centre), and *Walana* (right) are attending Stateship *Kabbarli*. Bottom left at B shed is State ship *Dulverton*, with HMAS *Diamantina* to her right and then *Dorrigo*. The *Centaur* can be seen across the harbour in front of the expanded grain silos.

Royalty

The SPHERE, London, April 17, 1954

XVII No. 2827

the SPHERE

with which is
incorporated
THE GRAPHIC

THE QUEEN SETS SAIL FROM AUSTRALIA—THE LINER "GOTHIC," CARRYING HER MAJESTY AND THE DUKE OF EDINBURGH, STEAMS AWAY FROM FREMANTLE AT THE CONCLUSION OF THE TWO-MONTH ROYAL TOUR OF THE COUNTRY : Many small craft are seen acting as an unofficial escort for the liner, while curtains of water cascade from the nozzles of a powerful fire-float. Thousands of Western Australians are massed all along the harbour walls and at other vantage points.

triumphant two-month Royal tour of the Commonwealth of
f Edinburgh sailed in the Gothic

to meet her escort of warships, the Queen broadcast her farewell message to Australia, saying that she hoped the visit had demonstrated that the Crown was a human link between all peoples who owed allegiance to her—" an allegiance of power of compulsion." After Australia the Royal tour
and then the voyage

Left: 1954 Royal tour. Because a poliomyelitis epidemic was sweeping Western Australia, the Queen and the Duke of Edinburgh stayed on board the Royal Yacht *Gothic* in Fremantle Harbour. Here the *Gothic* heads to sea to meet her escort of warships after a highly successful two month Royal tour, farewelled by the Governor-General Sir William Slim and the Prime Minister Robert Menzies. The *Gothic* was a 15,911 ton cargo passenger liner normally capable of carrying 85 first class passengers. In 1968 she suffered a major fire and was broken up in 1969.

Opposite: 1963 Royal visit of the Queen and Prince Phillip aboard the Royal Yacht *Britannia*. Here the Queen is inspecting a guard of honour given by junior recruits from HMAS *Leeuwin*, with the new Port Authority building under construction behind.

Opposite right: Boys spearfishing take a break to watch the departure of the Royal Yacht *Britannia*.

Opposite below: the Queen's bedroom and the drawing room aboard *Britannia*.

Passenger Terminal

Until the Fremantle passenger terminal was opened in 1960, ship passengers were offloaded into transit sheds. The new terminal initially catered for some 200,000 passengers a year, until a dramatic decline in the 70s with the advent of cheaper air fares.

Built in the Post War Modernist Style, it features parquetry flooring, large escalators, and Howard Taylor artwork. Refurbished between 2009 and 2011, it is today a survivor in a world of rapidly changing and relocating ports.

Hostesses in their red and white uniforms provided valuable information and made a striking impression. They were a welcome incursion into a mainly male port environment.

Flotta Lauro's popular *Angelina Lauro*, from the deck of the *Canberra*. *Angelina Lauro* began life as the MS *Oranje* with the Netherlands Line, served as a hospital ship for Australia during the war, and was refitted as *Angelina Lauro* in 1966 for Flotta Lauro Line. Taken off the Australian run in 1972, she was a cruise ship until becoming a total loss following a fire in 1979. The SS *Canberra* had an illustrious career with P&O from 1961 till 1997, and her role as a troopship during the 1982 Falklands War increased her popularity even further. Her maiden voyage in 1961 was to Australia, leaving Southampton with 2,238 passengers, including 750 migrants for Australia.

North Wharf No. 10 berth: The 1962 Commonwealth Games in Perth have concluded and visitors are farewelled. The *Johan Van Oldenbarnevelt*, in Fremantle as a floating hotel during the Games, retired from its round-the-world service after this visit. Colourful paper streamers provide a final link between friends and loved ones before departure. The use of streamers goes back many years, but environmental issues, fewer passenger ships, and shorter voyages nowadays mean that the tradition has largely disappeared.

Port Authority hostesses in their striking uniforms were effective ambassadors for the port, and on occasion travelled the State, as seen here with Vanda Ligovich alongside an MMA (MacRobertson Millar Airlines) plane and hostess.

The *Challenger*. Built in 1945 as a B class Fairmile and named *Maureen,* she was used by the Army for training and target towing. Fremantle Port Authority bought her in 1961 and converted her to an inspection vessel, and reception vessel for important visitors. The original *Challenger* had arrived 140 years earlier. On 25 April 1829, Captain Charles Fremantle's frigate anchored off Garden Island and was lucky not to sink upon arrival, highlighting the tricky access to Fremantle, unsolved until C.Y. O'Connor's creation of the inner harbour. Captain Fremantle wrote that he had asked the Master to set a buoy on a rock to guide the ship. But the Master steered straight for the rock and grounded the ship: "Never since I have been at sea have I witnessed anything to equal the carelessness and stupidity of the Master; he placed a buoy on a rock and then steered for the buoy and ran the ship immediately on it....The Master deserves to be hanged immediately."

VIPs

1966: Above, Her Majesty Queen Elizabeth, the Queen Mother boards the Fremantle Port's *Challenger*, escorted by Hon. Ross Hutchinson DFC MLA and his wife.
1980: Above right, Charles Court, Premier of Western Australia, farewells Governor of Western Australia Sir Wallace Kyle - Kalgoorlie born but retiring to Tiptoe in the UK.

1968: His Imperial Majesty Haile Selassie 1, Emperor of Ethiopia during a two day visit to Western Australia on May 16 and 17, 1968, being welcomed by The Hon G.C. MacKinnon, MLC, Minister for Health and Fisheries and Fauna, and Mrs MacKinnon. Aide-de-campe for the Australian visit, Wing Commander C.D. Bremner is in the centre. The Port Authority's inspection vessel *Challenger* was used to convey the Emperor to Perth.

Fishing Boat Harbour

Above: Blessing of the Fleet, Fishing Boat Harbour 1981. An animated and joyous, but respectful view by local artist Ian de Souza of an important annual event. Held since 1948 it heralds the start of the fishing and crayfishing seasons.
Opposite: Fishing Boat Harbour 1962. A dynamic and moody view of a sheltering fleet.

Kangaroos
and Elephants

Above left: Skippy and Ed Devereaux
c1967 with port hostess Pauline
Auguste. *Skippy the Bush Kangaroo* was
an Australian television series
produced between 1966 and 1968.
Left: 1963: Elephant being unloaded
on North Wharf on 24 January for the
Perth Zoo. Jumbo was one of two
elephants bought from Malaya. The
crowd is allowed to get surprisingly
close to proceedings.

c1960 view across the Bridge Hotel and Tilleys' boatsheds. Near the hotel, large port related sheds are moving in and squeezing out residences.

Containers

1964: *Kooringa* (above) - believed to be the world's first purpose-built container ship, in Fremantle. At 5,825 tons, she was equipped with two portable gantry cranes, with a capacity of 704 three-ton containers for the Fremantle to Melbourne run. On February 22, 1962, Premier David Brand opened a new sea-freight terminal at North Fremantle. Since 1958, because of lowered charges being offered by road and rail, three-ton containers had been introduced to try to improve efficiency and competitiveness. The benefits of no pilfering, more protection, and cheaper insurance soon became evident. Conventional ships spent one third of their lives in port, and the advent of containers greatly speeded up the whole cargo handling process. In July 1968, a 500 ton Portainer crane (left) is seen being installed at No. 12 berth, capable of lifting two 25 ton containers at a time.

1962: The 2,300 men aboard HMS *Ark Royal* enjoyed a 10 day visit. The 50,000 ton aircraft carrier was at that time the largest ship to enter Fremantle Harbour, but not the longest. HMS *Hood* visited Fremantle in 1924 and was 51 feet longer than the *Ark Royal*. The *Ark Royal* was launched in 1955. This floating airfield was decommissioned in 1979. At the passenger terminal across the river the *Kuala Lumpur* is berthed along with a Clan Line freighter. *Kuala Lumpur*, formerly the troopship *Dilwara*, could be configured for 1,669 pilgrims or 200 cruise passengers.

1962: HMAS *Anzac* with British submarine *Tapir,* and *Johan van Oldenbarnevelt* beyond. Grain silos being constructed behind.

Opposite: c1964 Vlase Zanalis' oil on masonite entitled *Success* features the new rail bridge which was relocated upstream near the traffic bridge, allowing the port to expand. Zanalis (1902-1973) had an interest in industry and labour, which is reflected in this painting. He spent weeks underground painting miners. He is best known for a series of eighty-eight paintings on Aboriginal subjects. This painting tells a positive story of a busy port. The cranes are almost talking to each other as they load the State's produce. Passenger ships bearing migrants sit watched over by the newly finished Port Authority building on the left. And, the small craft give a hint of recreation and prosperity.
Above: Flowers for lucky passengers at the new passenger terminal.

Above: Three Japanese whalers are in port and Ronnie Friessbourg (13) from Hilton Park shows Japanese whalers Hiroaki Atumi (right) and Yositaka Oyama, on December 22, 1962, a pigeon he caught on the wharf. Japanese whaling is today highly controversial.
Left: 1968 drilling rig *Jubilee*.
Opposite: Taiwanese frigates (left to right) *Hua Shan* (ex USS *Donald W. Wolf*), *Tai Yuan* (ex USS *Riley*), and destroyer *Keun Yang* (ex USS *Yarnall*) at No. 12 berth May 24, 1969.

1965: George Mackie with a large Kingfish caught in the harbour. It is a sad reflection on the altered health and wealth of the river that such catches are unlikely today. *Left:* General cargo ship *Awoshima Maru.*

December 7, 1969: HMAS *Quiberon* smashes a Harbour Trust carpenter's punt. Just three years later HMAS *Quiberon* was sold for scrap, for $68,260. So ended the long and distinguished career of an Australian destroyer. Commissioned in 1942, she sank the Italian submarine *Dessie* with the very first depth charges she fired. She rescued sailors from her sister ship HMS *Quentin* when she was sinking, though the captain had to leave behind four or five officers and ratings who had insisted on going below to get their belongings:"I cannot imagine how anyone might be so foolish," wrote the captain.

April 11, 1958: the interstate passenger ship *Kanimbla*. A typical *Kanimbla* cargo arriving at Fremantle included: 10 tons of jam, 10 tons of cheese, 71 tons of canned food, 60 tons of margarine, 5 tons of cigarettes, 330 tons of tyres, motor cars, 5 tons of nails, 25 tons of batteries, 50 tons of glass, and 35 tons of paint. *Kanimbla*'s maiden voyage to Fremantle was in 1936 with 195 passengers, though the 10,985 ton ship had a capacity of 400. Interestingly, between 1936 and 1939 she had an on-board radio broadcasting studio. During the war the ship had a stellar career as an armed RAN merchant cruiser.

Fine Lining

Opposite: Lloyd Triestino's *Guglielmo Marconi*, which, with sister ship *Galileo Galilei*, operated on the Italy to Australia run from 1963. In 1983 she became the *Costa Riviera* with Costa Cruises, until scrapped in 2002. *Right*: Orient Line's *Oriana*. When built in 1960, she was the biggest ship ever built in England. She could carry 628 First and 1,496 Tourist Class passengers at 30 knots.

1963: *Galileo Galilei* being brought in by the tug *Wyola* on her maiden voyage. Built for the Italy to Australia route, she was the flagship of the Lloyd Triestino line, a company founded in 1836. Gross tonnage was 27,800, with passenger accommodation for 1,677 and a speed of 27.3 knots (half loaded). *Galileo Galilei* was sold in 1983 and operated as a cruise ship until sinking in 1999 following an engine room fire.

1965: 35,000 ton RHMS *Australis*. Formerly the SS *America*, she was purchased by the Chandris Line and renamed *Australis*. A £3 million upgrade made the *Australis* the biggest one class ship afloat.

1966: *Caronia*, a Cunard White Star liner carrying 500 wealthy (American) tourists, arrives March 7. A fine quality ship only in service for nineteen years, the 34,183 ton *Caronia* was launched in 1948. A ship of fine brandy and cigars, it was said the cigars could be smelt before the ship docked. A notable event for this cruise ship occurred in 1958 when she demolished a lighthouse while sailing out of Yokohama.

One of the most evocative images taken in Fremantle Harbour, with no hint of the disaster that followed the next year. *Johan van Oldenbarnevelt* is seen arriving for the 1962 Commonwealth Games in Perth. The next year, after 33 years' service, the ship was renamed TSMS *Lakonia* and sailed from Southampton on December 19 for a "Christmas Cruise" to the Canary Islands with 1,022 people on board. Fire broke out due to defective electrical wiring and the ship was abandoned. The ship sank. 128 people died.

Above: Sitmar liner, *Castel Felice*. When she arrived in Fremantle on her maiden voyage on November 3, 1952, there were 1,390 Italians on board, 760 being assisted migrants. 218 disembarked in Fremantle instead of the intended 98, possibly because of a recent clash in Sydney between Italians and the police. By 1970, the ship had brought over 100,000 migrants to Australia.
Opposite: P&O's 29,734 ton *Arcadia*. When completed in 1954 she was the most expensive liner ever built in Britain. Sister ship *Iberia* was built the same year. Using six liners, P&O could offer a fortnightly service between the UK and Australia. Her distinctive yellow stack was designed to carry fumes and smut well aft of the ship to protect the decks and: "Women passengers are thus able to wear their best summer frocks without fear." When she arrived in Fremantle in 1954 on her maiden voyage she was the largest ship to visit Fremantle since the war. Those wishing to board the ship during her stay could get a permit.
On board were 14,000 sheets, 5,000 blankets, 10,000 dinner plates, 7,000 breakfast cups (but only 4,500 saucers), and 31,000 glasses.

RMHS *Ellinis* (opposite) in Fremantle in the early 1970s. This well-loved ship had a long career spanning almost 50 years. Beginning in 1932 as Matson Line's SS *Lurline*, she became a US naval transport in World War Two and took Prime Minister John Curtin to the USA to meet President Roosevelt in 1944. John Curtin, the Federal Member for Fremantle 1928-31 and 1934-45, had a heart attack a few months after his return and died the next year while in office. In 1963 the ship's capacity was increased and she became a 1,688 one-class passenger liner for Chandris. For some ten years *Ellinis* made regular line voyages to Australia.

On the right is P&O's SS *Canberra*. Built in the Harland and Wolff Belfast shipyard, with a launch date of March 16, 1960, the 45,250 ton ship was a very popular liner and later cruise ship. Passenger capacity was 549 First and 1,685 Tourist Class.

1960s view looking south from the Port Authority building across the West End to the Fishing Boat Harbour and Cockburn Sound. Left foreground is the Elder Smith & Co Ltd warehouse. The sheds and the General Manager's house to the right of the railway line have since been demolished. The house was also known as Government Cottage and was where G.V. McCartney, the port's General Manager, lived until his death just months after handing over to F.W.E. Tydeman. McCartney had a remarkable port-related career that spanned 50 years, beginning work at the Pier-Master's office at the time the Railway Department ran the port's cargo handling facilities on the Long Jetty. By 1929 he had the top job at the Fremantle Harbour Trust and kept it until he retired in May 1950. Also gone since the above photograph was taken is the spotting tower for the Arthur Head guns seen to the right of the 1831 Round House (which is not round).

The Blue Funnel Line *Centaur* followed an earlier *Centaur* sunk during World War Two, and replaced *Gorgon* and *Charon* on the Fremantle to Singapore service. Blue Funnel Line also ran the *Ulysses, Nestor, Anchises,* and *Ascanius* on the Australia to United Kingdon service. The *Ascanius* is shown on the postcard above. Configured to take general cargo along with passengers, the *Centaur* could carry 4,000 sheep and 40 cows northwards from Fremantle, and 700 cattle southwards on the return journey.

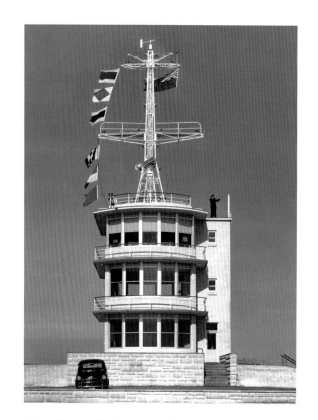

Above: Fremantle Port's signal station c1960.
Above left: Frank Manford Pty Ltd truck with a load of toys is checked at the Cliff Street exit gate c1968.
Left: Fremantle Port General Manager Frank Tydeman and his successor Hugh Rudderham outside the new Port Authority building c1965. Tydeman's 1949 report recommending upriver and seaward port expansion was overtaken by indications in 1953 that BP intended building an oil refinery at Kwinana. This triggered the rapid growth of the Outer Harbour. As General Manager 1950-1965, Tydeman oversaw increased mechanisation on the wharves, and a rebuilding program including the new passenger terminal and Port Authority building.
Opposite: 1965. Looking west down the Swan River over the 1939 timber traffic bridge with a new railway bridge just beyond it. The remains of the earlier railway bridge is further down river. The majestic wheat silos dominate the North Fremantle skyline. HMS *Bulwark*, commando carrier, is at North Wharf.

Above: Tug *Wilga* 1973, in the process of being decommissioned, though not during the lunch break. *Wilga* (Aboriginal for teeth) was UK built, and served in Britain's wartime merchant fleet, before coming to Fremantle in 1955. In 1973 there were five harbour tugs.

Frank Norton's delightfully positive realist modernist view of Fremantle Harbour in 1969 (right) reflects his passion for ships. An official war artist during World War Two for the RAN and RAAF, he authored several books on ships. He was appointed Director of the WA Art Gallery in 1958, a position he held until 1976. Major elements of the port and city are clearly depicted. *Centaur* is on its way out. At A berth is the Stateship *Kangaroo*.

FRANK NORTON

1970s

Right: 1970. Eager migrants clamber ashore after a lengthy voyage on Sitmar's one class liner *Fairsky*.

Opposite: Grain gantries ready to load as the *Uniwersytet Jagiellonski* comes in to berth, 1972.

Above: 80 ton floating crane *Pelican* alongside Shaw Savill passenger/cargo liner *Athenic*. *Athenic's* sister ship *Gothic* brought the Queen to Australia.
Opposite: Famous Australian industrial photographer Wolfgang Sievers was in Fremantle in 1977. Post World War Two, with his dramatic use of light showing the power of industry, Sievers helped alter Australia's image as a land of sheep and wool to one of industry and manufacturing.

Canadian 1973 built *Avon Forest* RO-RO (roll-on roll-off) cargo ship, built as a newsprint and vehicle carrier. Ice-strengthened for operation in the Great Lakes, she is here in Fremantle in 1979. 19,850 tons with a 2,250 car capacity, she became the *Cape Lambert* in 1987 when acquired by the US Fleet.

1989: USS *Midway* at F Berth during her 44th year of service in the US Navy. A few months before arriving in Fremantle, USS *Midway* was on standby following the Tiananmen Square massacre in case evacuation of US citizens from China was necessary. After the visit the carrier spent a week supporting the Philippine government of Corazon Aquino against a coup attempt. 45,000 tons when commissioned in 1945, she was 74,000 tons when decommissioned in 1992, due to several refits. 212,000 horsepower gave this leviathan a top speed of 33 knots. She consumed 100,000 gallons of oil a day. USS *Midway* lives on in San Diego where she is on display and ranked the number one attraction in the city.

Yachting

Fremantle and its port have played host to many yachting events, none more famous than the 1986 America's Cup. Opposite can be seen some of the huge crowd attending one race, in a view from the Port Authority building looking over what little remains of Arthur Head. The 2011 Fremantle to Bali race with 23 yachts entered, organised by the Fremantle Sailing Club, is seen above.

Gone fishing.

The world's most famous ocean liner departs Fremantle for the last time March 5, 2008. Launched in 1967, *Queen Elizabeth 2* sailed 5.6 million nautical miles, did 802 Atlantic crossings, and fitted in 24 full world cruises. By 2005 she became Cunard's longest serving liner, surpassing *Aquitania*'s 35 years.

Above left: Pilot boat *Parmelia*. *Left:* Pilot boat *Paddy Troy*. *Opposite:* The 69,153 ton four star *Oriana* and the 68,870 ton five star *Crystal Serenity* 2007. Appearances may be deceptive because the *Oriana* (right) is only 283 tons heavier than the *Crystal Serenity*. The trend towards providing more cabins with balconies has led to many box-like cruise ships. Despite their similar size, *Crystal Serenity* sails with half the number of passengers that the *Oriana* does.

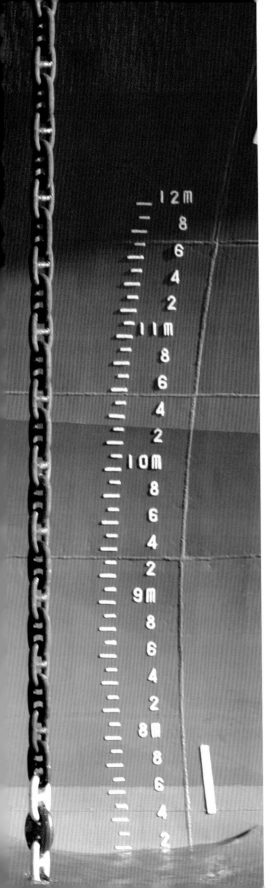

Top: 1955. January 11. The official opening of the Outer Harbour. First BP oil tanker *British Crusader* berths at Kwinana at Australia's first major lubricating oil complex.
Above: Upgraded Kwinana Bulk Terminal, acquired by FPA in 2002 from BHP Billiton.

Outer Harbour

Kwinana Bulk Jetty 2008. The Outer Harbour, about twenty kilometres to the south at Kwinana, is one of Australia's major bulk cargo ports handling grain, petroleum, liquid petroleum gas, alumina, mineral sands, fertilisers, coal, sulphur iron ore, and other bulk commodities. The State Government-owned port is a mix of facilities and services managed by Fremantle Ports and private operators. Three of the jetties in the Outer Harbour are operated by private companies, generally under Special Agreement Acts with the State. They are the Alcoa, BP Refinery, and CBH jetties. The Kwinana Bulk Jetty and the Kwinana Bulk Terminal are operated by Fremantle Ports.

Colourful port nightlife.

Bigger ships need taller cranes with longer outreach. On November 7, 2006, a huge new container crane was delivered to the Patrick container terminal on the Chinese heavy lift ship *Zhen Hua ll*, which was carrying five other cranes for further destinations in Australia and New Zealand. This was Fremantle Port's first post-Panamax crane and the discharge operation took four days to complete. Fremantle's second post-Panamax crane was delivered to the DP World container terminal on the March 31, 2010 in the same ship.

Since the Inner Harbour opened for business in 1897, the number of ship visits annually has only increased four fold. Contrastingly, the gross total tonnage of these vessels has increased 100 fold. After many years of exporting timbers, wool, gold, wheat and fisheries products, the main exports through Fremantle Port now are grain, alumina, refined petroleum, black coal, metal scrap, and animal feeds. Main imports are petroleum crude/refined, cement clinker, caustic soda, and phosphates.

A brisk July morning, 2011. Container trade set a record in 2010/11, with a total of 598,534 TEU (twenty foot equivalent units) handled, China being the major trading partner for containers.

Top: Indian Navy destroyer *Rana*, commissioned in 1982, departing Fremantle June 7, 2010, following a four day visit.
Above: B Shed, a 1926 general cargo shed, here adapted for use as a ferry terminal adjacent to O'Connor Landing.

Above: June 6, 2006 Mexican Navy sail training ship *Cuauhtemoc*. Commissioned in 1982. 1,662 tons and 268 crew.

Ships keep getting bigger, necessitating significant dredging programs like the $250 million deepening project in 2010. In 2009, MSC *Confidence* (above) became the first post-Panamax ship to enter Fremantle Port. The ship was unable to access the Inner Harbour fully loaded at that time.

A huge increase in cruising by Australians has seen some ships like *Sun Princess* (above) base themselves in Australia. Built in 1995 at a cost of $300 million, the 77,499 ton ship has a crew of 900 and a capacity of 2,250 passengers. A large and popular ship, but not so large compared with recent cruise ships like *Allure of the Seas* and *Oasis of the Seas*, both 225,282 tons and carrying 5,400 passengers each. Sailing the oceans of the world in 2011, there were 46 cruise ships over 100,000 tons each. All seem to have a mind-boggling array of facilities, activities, and unlimited food. Few however have the exterior style, grace, and attractive lines of earlier liners from the previous one hundred years.

MV *Tortugas*, car and truck carrier, with a capacity of 6,350 car units.

Fremantle Inner Harbour August, 2011.

Queen Mary 2

Queen Mary 2, the largest ship ever to enter the Inner Harbour, leaves Fremantle in March 2010. One of the Seven Wonders of the Waves, she is the first liner to be built for 40 years. Her bow was inspired by the 1935 *Normandie* and her funnel modelled on *QE2*. The ship has four whistles, one of them off the original *Queen Mary*.

Passengers consume 62,426 pounds of lobster a year, and the ship is the world's largest single customer for caviar.

With 150,000 gross tonnage and 157,000 horsepower, the ship can travel at 30 knots, and has a passenger capacity of 2,620.

Bibliography

Acknowledgements

Cairns, Lynne, *Fremantle's Secret Fleets*, WA Museum 1995

Davidson, Ron, *Fremantle Impressions*, FACP 2007

de Souza, Ian, *Reflective Impressions*, Reflective 2000

Dominions Royal Commission, *Royal Commission on the Natural Resources, Trade, and Legislation of Certain Portions of HM's Dominions,* HMSO 1913

Dowson, John, *Old Fremantle*, UWA Press 2003

Dowson, John, *Old Fremantle Childhood*, Fremantle 2006

Dowson, John, *Fremantle The Immigration Story*, Fremantle Society 2001

Fremantle History Society, *Fremantle Studies* Vols 1-6, FHS 1999-2010

Fremantle Harbour Trust, *Handbook of Information Relative to the Port of Fremantle 1935*, FHT, 1935

Fremantle Port Authority, *Port of Fremantle Quarterly Journal*, FPA 1961-

Evans, A.G., *C.Y. O'Connor His Life and Legacy*, UWA 2001

Herbert, Xavier, *Disturbing Element*, A&R 1963

Hutchings, P. & Lewis, J., *Kathleen O'Connor Artist in Exile*, FACP 1987

Le Page, J.S.H., *Building a State*, 1986

Millett, Mrs Edward, *An Australian Parsonage*, London 1872

Plowman, Peter, *Across the Sea to War*, Rosenberg 2003

Reece, Bob, *A Place of Consequence*, FACP 1983

Reece, Bob (ed.), *Early Days of Fremantle by J.K. Hitchcock*, Reece 2009

Trove: Online access to various newspapers

Tull, Malcolm, *Blood on the Cargo*, Labor History No. 52 1987

Tull, Malcolm, *A Community Enterprise, The History of the Port of Fremantle 1897-1997*, St. Johns 1997

This book would not have been possible without the significant help and support given by Fremantle Ports and its staff.

Fremantle Ports archivist Alan Pearce has been enormously helpful. Over recent years he has built an extensive photographic collection chronicling the port and has gone out of his way time and time again to help. Thanks also to Ainslie de Vos and Carol-Ann Huging, Fremantle Ports; Bruce Farrington, who has been studying the port for more than 50 years; Tim Lethorn, Tom Reynolds and staff at State Records Office; Battye Library; Alec Coles, Michael Gregg and Sally May from WA Museum; Fremantle Local History Library; Hugh Alexander, National Archives Kew; John Curtin Prime Ministerial Library; Earle Seubert, Grace Schultz, Robert Vallis, Helen Rocke, Geoffrey Higham, Jeff Austin, Janet Muir, Professor Reg Appleyard, Larry Foley, Doug Sellick, Ted Snell, Ron Davidson, Veronica Stratton and the family of Saxon Fogarty, David Cornelius, Helen Harvey, Andre Lipscombe, Andrew Pittaway, Ian and Rosslyn de Souza, Verna Townsend, Robert Grantham, Geoff Atterton, Bob Leggatt, Helen Birch, Rob O' Connor, Michael Adeane, and Desbye Shields.

Twenty years from now you will be more disappointed by the things you didn't do than by the ones you did. So throw off the bowlines. Sail away from the safe harbour. Catch the trade winds in your sails. Mark Twain

The Images

Page number is given first, followed by the name of the image, then owner. Following that is the catalogue number if any, and finally, if known, the photographer or artist's name in brackets. Abbreviations: Battye (Battye Library Perth), FPA (Fremantle Ports Collection), SRO (State Records Office), RWAHS (Royal Western Australian Historical Society), WAN (Western Australian Newspapers), Freo (Fremantle Local History Collection, Fremantle Library), WAM (Western Australian Museum), NLA (National Library of Australia), AWM (Australian War Memorial), Kew (National Archives, Kew, UK), Freo Art (Fremantle Council Art Collection), NT (Northern Territory Library), NA (National Archives), JCPML (John Curtin Prime Ministerial Library).

Dust jacket: Aerial by C. Meek, SRO PWD3796
1. Wet Wharf, WAN Freo 167
2. *Queen Mary 2*, Dowson (Dowson)
3. Early Arrival, Dowson (Fred Flood)
4. Early Arrival, Dowson (Fred Flood); High-nich and Newborn, (D.Chabanne and S. Allen)
5. Cat Resting, NT 0831/0092, (Syd Cuffe)
6. 1865 Map, RWAHS
7. 1865 Map, RWAHS
8. 1878 Lighthouse, RWAHS AR1986-130
10-11. 1870 High Street, Battye 100025PD and 100029PD
12-13. 1870 South Bay, Battye 100052PD and 100053PD
14-15. Various Plans (Acc 1647, items 884, 892, 910, 11219, 11219 plan 2, 11219 plan 3, 2221, 26375 Drawing 1), SRO
16-17. Browne plans, SRO 1647/11219 (Thomas Browne)
18. Long Jetty c1905, Battye 009630PD (Passey)
19. Camels on Long Jetty c1905, Battye 017558PD (Passey)
20. 1870 High Street (detail), Battye 100025PD;

River View, Battye 010722D
21. Rous Head, RWAHS R3015
22. Passmore Embroidery, WAM PH8604-046
24. The Bar, Dowson
25. View from Town Hall, Battye 100060PD
26. Forsyth's boat WAM MH644-P002
27. Coode v O'Connor, SRO Acc1647/15605
28. Harbour Works, SRO Cons 1647/5868-2
30. Blasting the bar, Freo 1799; Harbour construction, Battye 3542B/36
31. Victoria Quay, Rocke (Hodgson); Tender Penguin, Freo 1793
32. Pile Driving, Battye 3542B/36, 980P
33. Waterfront, Stephen O'Brien (Edward Wharton White); O'Connor House, Fremantle Arts Centre Press
34. Fremantle Bridge, Kew CO1069-626 (4)
35. Dredging (top) Freo 1800; Dredge Silhouette Freo 305 (Izzy Orloff)
36. Wharf 1899, Appleyard (Nixon & Merrilees)
37. Swan River 1893, Battye BA1116/10
38. Fremantle Harbour in the Making, RWAHS R001-003 Album N
39. Pile Driving, Battye 3972B/2
40-41. Open for Business (1904), Battye 5213P (Melvin Vaniman)
42. *Saida* (2), Helen Harvey
43. Warship 1903, Battye 013287D (Passey)
44. Group on deck, Battye 006643PD (Passey)
45. SS *Perth*, Battye 006430PD (Passey)
46. Power House, Battye 006008PD (Passey)
47. Harbour Entrance, Battye 3542B/35 (A.Pick-

ering)
48. Harbour Works, SRO Cons 1647/15300-2
49. Wool Transport, Kathleen Cant (nee Daly); Moving office, Battye 862B
50. Wharf, Battye 225578P (A. Pickering)
51. *Awhina*, Battye 017559PD (Passey)
52. Lumper Wiping Brow, FPA
53. Loading timber, Battye 009666PD (Passey)
54-55 Sandalwood(4) Freo; Sandalwood on Crane, Battye 10136P
56. Loading sandalwood 1907, Battye 010128PD (Rome, E.G.)
57. *Yongala*, Battye 010416PD; *Yongala* postcard, Dowson
58. *Grosser Kurfurst*, Battye 006426PD
59. *Grosser Kurfurst*, Wikmedia Commons
60. HMS *Powerful*, Battye 009623PD (Passey)
61. Pumping Water, Max Grunberg (Norman Lindsay); Postcard of wharf, Battye 441B (James Shaw)
62. Boys on wharf, Linton (Arnold Beste); Loading Daimler, (FM Robinson)
63. Fishing on wharf, Battye 008108PD (Passey)
64-65 Orient Line 1889 Schedule, Dowson; RMS *Moldavia*, Battye 009563PD (Passey)
66. *Queen Margaret*, Rocke (Hodgson)
67. Entering Fremantle Harbour, Smithsonian Institution, Division of Work and Industry, National Museum of American History 2004-9646 (Fred Taylor)
68. Railway Bridge, Battye 006409PD (cropped) (Passey)

The Images continued

69. Railway Yard, Battye 009244PD (Passey)
70. Troops Embarking, AWM H16159
71. Wounded Return, AWM H16167; Fremantle Gratefully Welcomes You, Dowson
72. Wheat, Battye 031192PD, 031197PD, 031188PD
73. Wheat, Battye 031189PD
74. Fishermen, Battye 006491PD
75. Italian Fishing Boats, Battye 112376PD (Izzy Orloff)
76. William Renton, JCPML 00830/175/57; Tom Edward's Funeral 00830/175/5377
77. Lumpers, Battye 111955PD, 12286D (both Izzy Orloff)
78. Alex McCallum, JCPML 00830/169; SS *Karoola*, Battye 111768PD (Izzy Orloff)
79. HMS *Hood*, Battye 111889PD (Izzy Orloff); HMS *Hood*, Battye 112349PD (Izzy Orloff)
80. HMS *Renown* (detail), Dowson (Kretchmar), Souvenir Programme, Dowson
81. Royal Couple, Battye 112428PD; Aerial of HMS *Renown*, Dowson
82. *Almkerk* 1927, Battye 047426PD ; Metro Bus, Battye 047477PD
83. Cofferdam, Christine Foulkes-Taylor (Cyril Morgan)
84. *Coming Alongside,* Dowson (Fred Flood)
85. *Early Arrival*, Dowson (Fred Flood)

86. Naval Ships, WAN FLD95 (Fred Flood)
87. *Empress of Britain*, WANSHIP254/COM213
88. Wharf Embarkation, Battye 046891PD
89. Off to War, Battye 046912PD
90. Troopships (cropped), AWM 029140; Troopship Convoy Anchored, AWM 000631
91. *Sontay*, Battye BA597/62; Bomb Poster, Freo
92. *Queen Mary*, AWM 303830; Menus, Dowson
93. Loading Money, AWM 029170; Gym and Pool, Souvenir Number *The Shipbuilder* June 1936, Dowson
94. *Aquitania* tender, Battye 226628PD;
95. Shipbuilder, Dowson
96-101. *Aquitania* fold out and glass slides, Dowson
102. Girl Signalling, Battye 006792D
103. Subs at North Wharf, Veronica Stratton (Saxon Fogarty)
104. MV *Panamanian* on Fire, Battye 221123PD; MV *Panamanian*, Veronica Stratton (Saxon Fogarty)
105. Victoria Quay c1946, WAN SHIPS823
106. British Family, Battye 221123PD
107. Migrants Arriving, Veronica Stratton (Saxon Fogarty)
108-109. Port Panorama, Veronica Stratton (Saxon Fogarty)

110. Swans in River, WAM 4593/15; Loading Fruit, Earle Seubert (Frank Slee)
111. *Mundalla* in Port, WAN C8356
112. Aerial looking west, NLA 23162138 (Frank Hurley)
113. Aerial looking east, NLA 23162058 (Frank Hurley)
114. Aerial looking south, NLA 23162017 (Frank Hurley)
115. Aerial looking north, NLA 23817464 (Frank Hurley)
116. Russian Research vessel, FPA; Grain facility, WAN B11
117. Port Panorama, FPA
118. *The Sphere*, Dowson
119. Queen Inspecting Sailors, FPA; *Britannia* Departs, WAN Q1304; *Britannia* Queen's Bedroon, Dowson (Dowson), Drawing Room, Dowson (Dowson)
120. Hostess and *Orsova*, FPA
121. Passenger Terminal, FPA
122. View of Passenger Terminal, Battye 214290PD
123. 1962 Departure, FPA
124. Hostesses, FPA
125. MV *Challenger,* FPA
126. Queen Mother, FPA; Governor Farewelled, FPA
127. Emperor Selassie, FPA
128. Fishing Boat Harbour, NA 11845045

Index

to be continued....